What people are saying about

# Pagan Portals – Aphrodite

Irisanya Moon's passion for and knowledge of Aphrodite shines through in this book which is a beautiful mosaic of compelling personal stories, research and hands on tools. Aphrodite: Encountering the Goddess of Love & Beauty & Initiation, shows us that the Greek Goddess of Love is far more multi-faceted than she is typically made out to be. The author provides the reader with a multitude of techniques for getting to know Aphrodite better, including methods for writing personal devotional chants, altar and offering ideas, and powerful immersive exercises. This book is a treasure for both long time Aphrodite devotees and those just beginning to hear the call of the Goddess of Love.
**Robin Corak**, author of *Persephone: Practicing the Art of Personal Power*

Irisanya brings her own personal interactions along with the ancient myths and stories of this fascinating goddess. Full of interesting details and suggestions on how to work with this many faceted goddess, this book is a must have for anyone wishing to embark on a journey with Aphrodite.
**Rachel Patterson**, author of *Moon Magic, The Cailleach* and the Kitchen Witchcraft series

Pagan Portals

# Aphrodite

Encountering the Goddess of Love
& Beauty & Initiation

Pagan Portals
# Aphrodite

Encountering the Goddess of Love
& Beauty & Initiation

Irisanya Moon

MOON
BOOKS

Winchester, UK
Washington, USA

JOHN HUNT PUBLISHING

First published by Moon Books, 2020
Moon Books is an imprint of John Hunt Publishing Ltd., No. 3 East Street, Alresford
Hampshire SO24 9EE, UK
office@jhpbooks.net
www.johnhuntpublishing.com
www.moon-books.net

For distributor details and how to order please visit the 'Ordering' section on our website.

Text copyright: Irisanya Moon 2019

ISBN: 978 1 78904 347 1
978 1 78904 348 8 (ebook)
Library of Congress Control Number: 2019948223

A CIP catalogue record for this book is available from the British Library.

Design: Stuart Davies

UK: Printed and bound by CPI Group (UK) Ltd, Croydon, CR0 4YY
US: Printed and bound by Thomson-Shore, 7300 West Joy Road, Dexter, MI 48130

We operate a distinctive and ethical publishing philosophy in
all areas of our business, from our global network of authors to
production and worldwide distribution.

# Contents

# Acknowledgements

I want to thank and presence the love in my life. I thank my partner, my husband, and my best friend, J. I thank the friends who have loved me no matter the season or situation. I thank them for holding me, for showing up, and for pushing back when I needed a nudge. I thank the Reclaiming tradition for the home I have found in it and the priestess I have become because of experience, training, and beloved ones. And I thank Trevor Greenfield at Moon Books for believing in my ability to translate my love for Aphrodite into a book.

But I thank Aphrodite most of all. Thank you for holding me during this journey, for showing up during the times of doubt and hesitation. Thank you for pointing out what I needed to say and what I didn't need to say. Thank you for reminding me that the personal relationship we have is one that is sacred, but it could also inspire others to the love that I have only known because of you. Thank you Golden One for showing up right when I needed you, right when you held the mirror to my face and showed me the beauty that I am. I sing your praises and say your name proudly.

Aphrodite, Aphrodite, Aphrodite
Αφροδιτη, Αφροδιτη, Αφροδιτη

# Author's Note

In a world that seems so ugly at times, Aphrodite is a refreshing balm. I see Her as the waves that rush over rock, smoothing and shining each stone. Before, I gave into the way society makes beauty sound like a superficial waste of time. I dismissed it, mocked it, and walked away from all things that were not 'productive.'

But beauty for the sake of beauty is necessary, vital, and healing. Beauty invites wonder. Beauty reminds us of hope and possibility. Beauty gives us permission to stop, rest, and restore our tired bones. When all is confusing or brittle, beauty is softness. When all is heavy and tense, beauty is release. When all seems lost, beauty can call us home. And Aphrodite reminds us that in our beauty and in our ability to find and celebrate it, we are smoothed and we become resilience. For what can another do if we are truly and madly in love with the world?

Aphrodite, sweet one, dear one, beloved, I am blessed to know you, to honor you, and to dip my toes in the sand with you. May I hold you well. May you inspire more love and more hearts. May you look deeply into the eyes of another and let them know and trust themselves. Look deeper, look longer, and know.

I hold Aphrodite as a goddess who continues to unfold and emerge in response to the world. My interpretation and interaction with Her is modern, evolving, and personal. I invite you to find Her as you see Her too.

*(Note: I use "godd" as a more gender-inclusive term and "godds" as a plural noun. I also use capitalized She and Her when speaking of Aphrodite specifically.)*

# Hymn 5 to Aphrodite

Αφροδιτη (Greek) | Aphrodite (Latin) |
Aphroditê (Transliteration)
English Translation by Hugh G. Evelyn-White. Homeric
Hymns. Cambridge, MA., Harvard University Press; London,
William Heinemann Ltd. 1914.

## To Aphrodite

*[1] Muse, tell me the deeds of golden Aphrodite the Cyprian, who stirs up sweet passion in the gods and subdues the tribes of mortal men and birds that fly in air and all the many creatures [5] that the dry land rears, and all that the sea: all these love the deeds of rich-crowned Cytherea.*

*Yet there are three hearts that She cannot bend nor yet ensnare. First is the daughter of Zeus who holds the aegis, bright-eyed Athena; for She has no pleasure in the deeds of golden Aphrodite, [10] but delights in wars and in the work of Ares, in strifes and battles and in preparing famous crafts. She first taught earthly craftsmen to make chariots of war and cars variously wrought with bronze, and She, too, teaches tender maidens in the house [15] and puts knowledge of goodly arts in each one's mind. Nor does laughter-loving Aphrodite ever tame in love Artemis, the huntress with shafts of gold; for She loves archery and the slaying of wild beasts in the mountains, the lyre also and dancing and thrilling cries [20] and shady woods and the cities of upright men. Nor yet does the pure maiden Hestia love Aphrodite's works. She was the first-born child of wily Cronos and youngest too, by will of Zeus who holds the aegis, —a queenly maid whom both Poseidon and Apollo sought to wed. [25] But She was wholly unwilling, nay, stubbornly refused; and touching the head of father Zeus who holds the aegis, She, that fair goddess, swear a great oath which has in truth been fulfilled, that She would be a maiden all Her days. So Zeus the Father gave Her an high honor instead of marriage, [30] and She has Her place in the midst of the house and has the richest portion. In all the temples of the gods She has a share of honor, and among all mortal men She is chief of the goddesses.*

*Of these three Aphrodite cannot bend or ensnare the hearts. But of all others there is nothing [35] among the blessed gods or among mortal men that has escaped Aphrodite. Even the heart of Zeus, who delights in thunder, is led astray by Her; though he is greatest of all and has the lot of highest majesty, She beguiles even his wise heart whensoever She pleases, and mates him with mortal women, [40] unknown to Hera, his sister and his wife, the grandest far in beauty among the deathless goddesses —most glorious is She whom wily Cronos with Her mother Rhea did beget: and Zeus, whose wisdom is everlasting, made Her his chaste and careful wife.*

*[45] But upon Aphrodite herself Zeus cast sweet desire to be joined in love with a mortal man, to the end that, very soon, not even She should be innocent of a mortal's love; lest laughter-loving Aphrodite should one day softly smile and say mockingly among all the gods [50] that She had joined the gods in love with mortal women who bare sons of death to the deathless gods, and had mated the goddesses with mortal men.*

*And so he put in Her heart sweet desire for Anchises who at that time among the steep hills of many-fountained Ida [55] was tending cattle, and in shape was like the immortal gods. Therefore, when laughter-loving Aphrodite saw him, She loved him, and terribly desire seized Her in Her heart. She went to Cyprus, to Paphos, where Her precinct is and fragrant altar, and passed into Her sweet-smelling temple. [60] There She went in and put to the glittering doors, and there the Graces bathed Her with heavenly oil such as blooms upon the bodies of the eternal gods —oil divinely sweet, which She had by Her, filled with fragrance. And laughter-loving Aphrodite put on all Her rich clothes, [65] and when She had decked herself with gold, She left sweet-smelling Cyprus and went in haste towards Troy, swiftly travelling high up among the clouds. So She came to many-fountained Ida, the mother of wild creatures and went straight to the homestead across the mountains. After Her [70] came grey wolves, fawning on Her, and grim-eyed lions, and bears, and fleet leopards, ravenous for deer: and She was glad in heart to see them, and put desire in their breasts, so that they all mated, two together, about the shadowy coombes.*

*[75] But She herself came to the neat-built shelters, and him She found left quite alone in the homestead —the hero Anchises who was comely as the gods. All the others were following the herds over the grassy pastures, and he, left quite alone in the homestead, [80] was roaming hither and thither and playing thrillingly upon the lyre. And Aphrodite, the daughter of Zeus stood before him, being like a pure maiden in height and mien, that he should not be frightened when he took heed of Her with his eyes. Now when Anchises saw Her, he marked Her well and wondered at [85] Her mien and height and shining garments. For She was clad in a robe out-shining the brightness of fire, [89] a splendid robe of gold, enriched with all manner of needlework, which shimmered like the moon [90] over Her tender breasts, a marvel to see. Also She wore twisted brooches and shining earrings in the form of flowers; [87] and round Her soft throat were lovely necklaces. [88]*

*And Anchises was seized with love, and said to Her: [91] "Hail, lady, whoever of the blessed ones you are that are come to this house, whether Artemis, or Leto, or golden Aphrodite, or high-born Themis, or bright-eyed Athena. [95] Or, maybe, you are one of the Graces come hither, who bear the gods company and are called immortal, or else one of the Nymphs who haunt the pleasant woods, or of those who inhabit this lovely mountain and the springs of rivers and grassy meads. [100] I will make you an altar upon a high peak in a far seen place, and will sacrifice rich offerings to you at all seasons. And do you feel kindly towards me and grant that I may become a man very eminent among the Trojans, and give me strong offspring for the time to come. As for my own self, [105] let me live long and happily, seeing the light of the sun, and come to the threshold of old age, a man prosperous among the people."*

*Thereupon Aphrodite the daughter of Zeus answered him: "Anchises, most glorious of all men born on earth, know that I am no goddess: why do you liken me to the deathless ones? [110] Nay, I am but a mortal, and a woman was the mother that bare me. Otreus of famous name is my father, if so be you have heard of him, and he reigns over all Phrygia rich in fortresses. But I know your speech well beside my own, for a Trojan nurse brought me up at home: [115] She took me from my dear mother and reared me thenceforth when I was a little child. So comes it, then, that I well know your tongue also. And now the Slayer of Argus with the golden wand has caught me up from the dance of huntress Artemis, Her with the golden arrows. For there were many of us, nymphs and marriageable maidens, [120] playing together; and an innumerable company encircled us: from these the Slayer of Argus with the golden wand rapt me away. He carried me over many fields of mortal men and over much land untilled and unpossessed, where savage wild-beasts roam through shady coombes, [125] until I thought never again to touch the life-giving earth with my feet. And he said that I should be called the wedded wife of Anchises, and should bear you goodly children. But when he had told and advised me, he, the strong Slayer of Argos, went back to the families of the deathless gods, [130] while I am now come to you: for unbending necessity is upon me. But I beseech you by Zeus and by your noble parents —for no base folk could get such a son as you —take me now, stainless and unproved in love, and show me to your father and careful mother [135] and to your brothers sprung from the same stock. I shall be no ill-liking daughter for them, but a likely. Moreover, send a messenger quickly to the swift-horsed Phrygians, to tell my father and my sorrowing mother; and they will send you gold in plenty and woven stuffs, many splendid gifts; [140] take these as bride-piece. So do, and then prepare the sweet marriage that is honorable in the eyes of men and deathless gods."*

When She had so spoken, the goddess put sweet desire in his heart. And Anchises was seized with love, so that he opened his mouth and said:

[145] "If you are a mortal and a woman was the mother who bare you, and Otreus of famous name is your father as you say, and if you

*are come here by the will of Hermes the immortal Guide, and are to be called my wife always, then neither god nor mortal man [150] shall here restrain me till I have lain with you in love right now; no, not even if far-shooting Apollo himself should launch grievous shafts from his silver bow. Willingly would I go down into the house of Hades, O lady, beautiful as the goddesses, once I had gone up to your bed."*

*[155] So speaking, he caught Her by the hand. And laughter-loving Aphrodite, with face turned away and lovely eyes downcast, crept to the well-spread couch which was already laid with soft coverings for the hero; and upon it lay skins of bears and deep-roaring lions [160] which he himself had slain in the high mountains. And when they had gone up upon the well-fitted bed, first Anchises took off Her bright jewelry of pins and twisted brooches and earrings and necklaces, and loosed Her girdle and stripped off Her bright garments [165] and laid them down upon a silver-studded seat. Then by the will of the gods and destiny he lay with Her, a mortal man with an immortal goddess, not clearly knowing what he did.*

*But at the time when the herdsmen drive their oxen and hardy sheep back to the fold from the flowery pastures, [170] even then Aphrodite poured soft sleep upon Anchises, but herself put on Her rich raiment. And when the bright goddess had fully clothed herself, She stood by the couch, and Her head reached to the well-hewn roof-tree; from Her cheeks shone unearthly beauty [175] such as belongs to rich-crowned Cytherea. Then She aroused him from sleep and opened Her mouth and said:*

*"Up, son of Dardanus! —why sleep you so heavily? —and consider whether I look as I did when first you saw me with your eyes."*

*[180] "So She spake. And he awoke in a moment and obeyed Her. But when he saw the neck and lovely eyes of Aphrodite, he was afraid and turned his eyes aside another way, hiding his comely face with his cloak. Then he uttered winged words and entreated Her:*

*[185] "So soon as ever I saw you with my eyes, goddess, I knew that you were divine; but you did not tell me truly. Yet by Zeus who holds the aegis I beseech you, leave me not to lead a palsied life among men,*

but have pity on me; [190] for he who lies with a deathless goddess is no hale man afterwards."

Then Aphrodite the daughter of Zeus answered him: "Anchises, most glorious of mortal men, take courage and be not too fearful in your heart. You need fear no harm from me [195] nor from the other blessed ones, for you are dear to the gods: and you shall have a dear son who shall reign among the Trojans, and children's children after him, springing up continually. His name shall be Aeneas, because I felt awful grief in that I laid me in the bed of a mortal man: [200] yet are those of your race always the most like to gods of all mortal men in beauty and in stature.

Verily wise Zeus carried off golden-haired Ganymedes because of his beauty, to be amongst the Deathless Ones and pour drink for the gods in the house of Zeus — [205] a wonder to see —,honored by all the immortals as he draws the red nectar from the golden bowl. But grief that could not be soothed filled the heart of Tros; for he knew not whither the heaven-sent whirlwind had caught up his dear son, so that he mourned him always, unceasingly, [210] until Zeus pitied him and gave him high-stepping horses such as carry the immortals as recompense for his son. These he gave him as a gift. And at the command of Zeus, the Guide, the slayer of Argus, told him all, and how his son would be deathless and unageing, even as the gods. [215] So when Tros heard these tidings from Zeus, he no longer kept mourning but rejoiced in his heart and rode joyfully with his storm-footed horses.

So also golden-throned Eos rapt away Tithonus who was of your race and like the deathless gods. [220] And She went to ask the dark-clouded Son of Cronos that he should be deathless and live eternally; and Zeus bowed his head to Her prayer and fulfilled Her desire. Too simple was queenly Eos: She thought not in Her heart to ask youth for him and to strip him of the slough of deadly age. [225] So while he enjoyed the sweet flower of life he lived rapturously with golden-throned Eos, the early-born, by the streams of Ocean, at the ends of the earth; but when the first grey hairs began to ripple from his comely head and noble chin, [230] queenly Eos kept away from his bed, *though She cherished him in Her house and nourished him with food and ambrosia and gave him rich clothing. But when loathsome old age pressed full upon him, and he could not move nor lift his limbs, [235] this seemed to Her in Her heart the best counsel: She laid him in a room and put to the shining doors. There he babbles endlessly, and no more has strength at all, such as once he had in his supple limbs.*

*I would not have you be deathless among the deathless gods [240] and live continually after such sort. Yet if you could live on such as now you are in look and in form, and be called my husband, sorrow would not then enfold my careful heart. But, as it is, harsh old age will soon enshroud you — [245] ruthless age which stands someday at the side of every man, deadly, wearying, dreaded even by the gods.*

*And now because of you I shall have great shame among the deathless gods henceforth, continually. For until now they feared my jibes and the wiles by which, or soon or late, [250] I mated all the immortals with mortal women, making them all subject to my will. But now my mouth shall no more have this power among the gods; for very great has been my madness, my miserable and dreadful madness, and I went astray out of my mind [255] who have gotten a child beneath my girdle, mating with a mortal man. As for the child, as soon as he sees the light of the sun, the deep-breasted mountain Nymphs who inhabit this great and holy mountain shall bring him up. They rank neither with mortals nor with immortals: [260] long indeed do they live, eating heavenly food and treading the lovely dance among the immortals, and with them the Sileni and the sharp-eyed Slayer of Argus mate in the depths of pleasant caves; but at their birth pines or high-topped oaks [265] spring up with them upon the fruitful earth, beautiful, flourishing trees, towering high upon the lofty mountains (and men call them holy places of the immortals, and never mortal lops them with the axe; but when the fate of death is near at hand, [270] first those lovely trees wither where they stand, and the bark shrivels away about them, and the twigs fall down, and at last the life of the Nymph and of the tree leave the light of the sun together. These Nymphs shall keep my son with them and rear him, and as soon as he is come to lovely boyhood, [275] the goddesses will bring him here to you and show you your child. But, that I may tell you all that I have in mind, I will come here again towards the fifth year and bring you my son. So soon as ever you have seen him —a scion to delight the eyes —, you will rejoice in beholding him; for he shall be most godlike: [280] them bring him at once to windy Ilion. And if any mortal man ask you who got your dear son beneath Her girdle, remember to tell him as I bid you: say he is the offspring of one of the flower-like Nymphs [285] who inhabit this forest-clad hill. But if you tell all and foolishly boast that you lay with rich-crowned Aphrodite, Zeus will smite you in his anger with a smoking thunderbolt. Now I have told you all. Take heed: [290] refrain and name me not, but have regard to the anger of the gods."*

*When the goddess had so spoken, She soared up to windy heaven.*

*Hail, goddess, queen of well-builded Cyprus! with you have I begun; now I will turn me to another hymn.*

Some nameless one calls out to Aphrodite, calls out to Her and to Her wisdom. And thus, so do we.

# Introduction

Aphrodite and I were never meant to get along. From the time I understood that deity was a thing that could call to me, I dismissed any deity that looked like a fragile, unintelligent being. I didn't want to work with or be called by anyone who reminded me of a soft and unfocused version of myself.

I told myself that Aphrodite was a caricature of self-love and a shadow of what She could be. But even as I said that, I was taking a step toward Her. Without realizing it, my doubts were the steps toward understanding. I was already finding what intrigued me about Her. And, honestly, I realized the things that mystified me about myself.

For when I looked at the way that Aphrodite appeared soft, I began to know my own hardness. When I looked at the way She was 'always' doing things that were pleasurable, I began to notice the ways I wasn't inviting that into my life. When I judged Her for what others said, I realized I was also judging myself too harshly, without giving myself a chance or another opportunity to reveal the truth of where I was at.

In short, in dismissing Aphrodite, I was dismissing myself. And once I invited Her into my life (well, She sort of came in without a lot of inviting), I began to know those parts of myself that I had long dismissed and discounted. I began to understand and appreciate and know the ways in which things are more complicated, more nuanced, more delicate. Not fragile.

This is not to say that my work and relationship with Aphrodite has been easy, smooth, or even painless. While She might be known as the goddess of love and beauty and sexuality and even fertility, She is also the initiator, the jealous one, and often misunderstood. She is also an instigator, a troublemaker, and a being who wants what She wants when She wants it. I relate there too.

I am writing this book not as an expert or a human that knows the godds more than anyone else. I am fully aware that my relationship with Aphrodite is the lens through which I will talk about Her. And it might be wise to know that I hold the godds as part of myself and as separate entities and as unknowable beings – all at the same time. For at any moment, Aphrodite can be friend, challenger, and divine one who I bow to during prayers.

I am in a relationship with Her, to be sure. And She called me as clearly as someone may have called me for a first date or a slow dance. Hesitantly. Clearly. And I answered in only the way that one can in important moments – awkwardly, but with certainty. Yes. I will walk in this life with you. Yes, I will speak of you and celebrate you and cherish you. Yes, I will listen and wonder and question and make offerings to you. I will say your name until it rings in the ears of my world. I will sing your praises until the end of my days.

Hail Aphrodite.

# Chapter 1

# Encountering Aphrodite

To begin, I will start with where I met Her. Perhaps you have a story too or perhaps you didn't realize She was calling to you. I know I didn't realize it at first.

## A Personal Story / Call

I was at a large pagan gathering in San Jose, California: PantheaCon. During this event, groups and individuals apply to do presentations on any number of topics, traditions, deities, etc. In any given day during this almost five-day event, there are workshops and rituals happening and magick popping up at restaurant tables and hotel rooms.

And one year when I went, the weekend fell over Valentine's Day. Whether you believe this to be a day of celebration or misery, I'll leave you to that vision. But this weekend, the halls of the hotel were filled with love. I felt it in the air, in the presentations, and in the way that people engaged with each other. Gently.

Unsurprisingly, there were love rituals and one ritual that was in devotion to Aphrodite led by the Temple of Aphrodite. Though I wasn't overly interested in this ritual, I was curious and it sounded like fun. When I walked into the room, I knew the importance of the moment. I knew this was not only a time when I was going to learn, but it was a time that would change me.

To be fair, the details of what happened are a little vaguer today, many years later. But what I do remember is walking into the ritual and knowing myself to be one of Aphrodite's priestesses. At the beginning, there was a moment where we were dancing around and moving our bodies in sensual ways, and the priestesses of the ritual were giving golden beads to all who were present in the room.

These necklaces were given as the spirit moved those priestesses and everyone was 'chosen' by Aphrodite. But right at the end of this ritual piece, I was given another necklace. I looked around and no one else had two. And I was holding the other one in my hand, so it was clear that I was already 'chosen' before the second necklace arrived. It sounds silly, right? Even as I remember it, I think to myself how silly that is. I got two necklaces instead of one. It was a mistake, not a mystical experience. But I felt it. I felt it in my toes. I felt it in my fingertips.

Even as I write about it, I can feel my heart beating faster. I can feel the way I knew eyes to be on me at that moment – and they were not the eyes of the priestesses. The eyes of Her were fixed on me. I liken it to the story of Ereshkigal fixing the eye of death upon Inanna as She entered the Underworld. But in this case, Aphrodite fixed upon me the eye of life. The glance of love. The opening to vulnerability and never letting myself down again.

From that small, silly moment, I stepped toward Her and She stepped toward me. She filled my heart and my mind and my altar space. She held me and pushed me and looked deeply into my eyes to remind me that I was not alone. She held me with words, with songs, with the soft touch across my back.

## Meeting Again, Offering of Body and Bone

There was also the time She came to me in a workshop. I took a class on Aphrodite as part of a series of Courting the Goddess classes taught by Reclaiming teachers and lovers of Her. I had just had my 'moment' with Aphrodite, so I decided to start dating Her, so to speak. I wanted to get to know Her more. And while I could always read a book or do an internet search, I was more interested in being with others who already knew Her or who wanted to learn as I did.

We immersed ourselves in song, in writing love notes, and in the practice of aspecting the godds. Aspecting, in the Reclaiming tradition, is a form of possession work. In this practice, one opens themselves up to receive deity and to become a human vessel for a godd. In doing so, aspecting is an act of service and can be a practice of building relationships with deities.

When I was with my partner and asked to aspect Aphrodite, I remember Her coming into me, filling me with this iridescent light, and then I remember little after that. I remember that my partner was asking me questions. I remember my partner was smiling at me and holding my body, but the rest is vague.

As I came out of the aspecting, I felt my body be more alive and more awake than it had been. I felt as though some missing piece of myself had returned home. I also was clear that driving home was going to be a challenge after that experience.

A priestess told me that some deities like to linger in the tendons and the spaces between bones. I asked Aphrodite to leave and then I insisted that She leave. She did. But She then returned. She came to me in waves. She came to me as tiredness that pushes you into bed. I fell down for a day, wracked with the pain of loss (as I realize it now). I felt the ache of Her not being present and I was clear that I needed to invite Her in more, get to know Her more, and listen to Her. And so it began.

She comes to me on ocean waves, on whispers, and on the way that time sometimes stands still when you are so completely in the moment. She tells me that I cannot abandon myself. I need to be the lover of myself. I need to listen to the way that waves crash in a seashell, no matter how far away the ocean is. She brings me back to the shore of my own birth and realization. And there is nothing silly about that.

She has come to me in more intense ways and waves, in initiation and in the complication of this human experience. She shows up in the waters as often as She does in the sand. She arrives as a blessing – and sometimes as a reminder of how love is a wave, a motion, and sometimes a retreat. And She is also a mystery. She is also the fullness/emptiness of a heart and a relationship. She is the wonder and the waiting at the door for another kiss. Or the first kiss. Or the slowest goodbye because you truly don't want to see the other person leave.

## Beginning the Encounter

Whenever you decide to find a deity or to work with a particular energy, it can help to begin with curiosity. While there are stories and history books that will give you what is known about Aphrodite, personal experience is also true.

The relationship you have with a godd is completely up to you. You may find that Aphrodite is the softness you need or the strength you seek. You might find Her to be less of the seashell and more of a wave. You might come up with something completely different.

But all of this is based on experience and time. Just as we can't know a human instantly, the godds are not always clear in the way they present themselves to us. They may also need to take their time to get to know us. They might want to be clear about our intentions, and in doing so, offer wisdom and insight.

This is not to say that godds are always testing or suspicious – not in my experience, anyway. But some are. My relationship with Aphrodite has been different, softer, with a slower burn. It took time. It still takes time.

Perhaps in this moment, wherever you are, you might take a breath, take a moment to open yourself to Her presence and Her energy. Push aside what you have heard and allow your experience to be your own. Even as you read, trust your own feelings about what resonates and what does not. You will know Her in the way that you know Her.

One thing to keep in mind, Aphrodite is often noted as a virgin goddess, but not in the sense that you and I might think of this as being celibate. Instead, the word meant more of a being who is always remaining independent. 'One-in-herself' as Charlene Spretnak writes. May you too find what is already of yourself. Holy and true.

# Chapter 2

# The Birth of Aphrodite/Venus

To begin at the beginning is a common start of any relationship. We begin with the places we come from, the places we have been told we come from, and the places that we still call home. Aphrodite by the Greeks, Venus by the Romans, She stepped into the consciousness of the people, who eagerly awaited Her.

*"Aphrodite, Goddess of beauty, love, and desire, was an important deity on the Greek mainland from as early as the eighth century B.C. She was, however, a relative latecomer to the Greek Pantheon and widely considered by the ancient Greeks to be of Eastern origin. In the poems of Homer She is referred to as 'the lady of Kypros' (Cyprus), whose sacred precinct and smoky altar were located at Paphos. Hesiod describes Her birth from the mutilated genitals of Ouranos (Heaven) that were cast into the sea, creating white foam from which Aphrodite appeared before making landfall on the southwest corner of Cyprus. For Herodotus, Aphrodite was a Phoenician deity whose cult spread from Ascalon in Palestine to Cyprus and later to Greece, while Pausanias tells us that She was worshipped by the Assyrians, who passed on Her cult to the Phoenicians, who, in turn, transmitted it to Cyprus. Various theories on the original of Aphrodite have also been put forward in modern times, but the more recent scholarship leaves little doubt that She did indeed reach Greece from Cyprus."* – 'From Ishtar to Aphrodite: 3200 Years of Cypriot Hellenism' edited by Sophocles Hadjisavvas

But as with many godds, there are disputes about the story of Aphrodite, about Her family and Her birth. And perhaps there aren't clear conclusions to be made or maybe everything holds a small piece of truth.

We might be able to piece together our own translations of what happened, what was real and what was not, but in my relationship with Aphrodite, I am more interested in the energy she brings to Her seekers today. As such, I contextualize what I have read and what I have learned from a lens of my relationship and from what resonates with me. I invite you to do the same.

## The Sea Foam Birth

One of the more challenging parts of Aphrodite and the way She has been presented in the world is the story of Her birth. The most common story is that all began in Chaos. Gaia was born and She bore Uranus and with whom She conceived Oceanus and many daughters and sons. One of these sons was Cronos who held a deep hatred of his father Oceanus. Because Gaia too felt anger and resentment toward Uranus, She gave Cronos a sickle with which he cut off the genitals of his father and threw them into the sea. As the parts moved in the ocean, a white foam arose around them and in that foam (Aphros is foam, in Greek) a maiden grew and was carried to Cyprus: Aphrodite. It is said that once She stepped on the shore, flowers and green grass grew around Her feet.

Some have noted in this strange story that the time of love was only able to be born after a time of chaos. But when we look at this story, the only place it emerges is in 'Theogony' by Hesiod, so there is a question about its validity or perhaps its translation.

When we look at other texts, we begin to see that Aphrodite is also said to have come along in the waves of the ocean, carried to Cyprus. There are descriptions of Her wearing a golden crown, still being born of the sea foam. There She was greeted and gifted with heavenly garments to celebrate her arrival. The winds fled before Her and the storm clouds were pushed aside.

*"Aphrodite, Goddess of Desire, rose naked from the foam of the sea and, riding on a scallop shell, stepped ashore first on the island of Cythera; but finding this only a small island, passed on to the Peloponnese, and eventually took up residence in Paphos, in Cyprus, still the principal seat of her worship."* – 'The Greek Myths' by Robert Graves

And still another version of Her birth tells us that She is the daughter of Zeus and born from the partnering of him and Dione, an oracular goddess. And still other texts will call Her parents Ouranos and Hemera.

## The Challenge of Patriarchal Interpretation

One of the challenges with the stories available about deities is that they are subject to interpretation. Depending on the person who has offered a translation, we cannot be sure of the way the story is being told or why it is being told that way.

When looking back in history, there is a pattern of matriarchal societies that held histories that were then shifted when patriarchal societies took over. For example, the story of Demeter and Persephone did not always include a rape story. It was once the story of Persephone claiming her power as the Queen of the Underworld.

We could look at the story of Aphrodite's birth in the same way. Instead of being born of sea foam and true unto Herself, she becomes the product of violence against men. Perhaps this makes her image untrustworthy or dangerous, or at least one that could be questioned.

"Aphrodite is a fertility Goddess, the primal mother of all on-going creation. She is a virgin in the original sense (one-in-herself, not necessarily abstaining from sex but always remaining independent), and has eternal beauty. Her sea birth is yet another version (along with that of Pandora and

Persephone) of the anodos, the arising of the Goddess." – 'Lost Goddesses of Early Greece' by Charlene Spretnak

I would encourage ongoing study of where stories come from when looking at deities in general, and possibly especially in societies where power structures shifted. And it is worthy to note that many translators were men who may have had their own motives for making Aphrodite sound weak or somehow not as important as other godds. Or perhaps the storytellers were simply afraid of the Goddess arising.

I personally hold the story of a goddess who emerged from the sea because Her power was needed in the world. In a time of Chaos, it makes sense that a being of beauty and laughter was required. If that being had not emerged, what would be the point of the world continuing? What would be the point of the godds?

## The Family of Aphrodite

There are conflicting texts on what the family of Aphrodite looks like and who is part of the web that has been woven – or perhaps, better said, the waves upon which She was born. As before, Her parentage has a few different possibilities, but just as open to interpretation are her siblings and Her children. After all, it seems to be consistent in Greek mythos that there are many partnerings that lead to children.

Parents:

No parents – emerged from the sea fully formed or from the genitals of Uranus/Ouranos

Zeus and Dione

Ouranos and Hemera

Siblings:

Aeacus, Angelos, Apollo, Ares, Artemis, Athena, Dionysus,

Eileithyia, Enyo, Eris, Ersa, Hebe, Helen of Troy, Hephaestus, Heracles, Hermes, Minos, Pandia, Persephone, Perseus, Rhadamanthus, The Graces, The Horae, The Litae, The Muses, The Moirai / The Titans, The Cyclopes, The Meliae, The Erinyes (Furies), The Giants, The Hekatonkheires

Partners / Lovers:
Hephaestus, Ares, Poseidon, Hermes, Dionysus, Adonis, Anchises

Children with Ares:
Eros, Phobos, Deimos, Harmonia, Pothos, Anteros, Himeros

Children with Hermes:
Hermaphroditus

Children with Poseidon:
Rhodos, Eryx

Children with Dionysus:
Peitho, The Graces, Priapus

Children with Anchises:
Aeneas, Lyros

Children with Phaethon:
Astynoos

Children with the Argonaut Boutes:
Eryx

As you look at these lists, there is overlap and some siblings who also show up as children and siblings who show up as partners. It is a complicated web of connection. But the more we know of Aphrodite, the more we can begin to tease out the ways in which She has many facets and many more entry points for understanding.

## An Offering

What this might bring to mind as you begin to meet Aphrodite is the complication of family and potentially the complication of your own family experience. While this is typically not brought up as a common way to engage with Aphrodite, this exploration could offer a healing of the heart.

By moving through the stories of Aphrodite's family, you might find resonance. I offer the possibility that you might work with those stories in the following way. Find a story that resonates with you and read it carefully. Focus not on what you believe it to mean or how it impacted Aphrodite, but focus on the events, their order, and their outcome(s). Once you have the story in your mind, assemble a list of the characters in the story.

Move through the story again as each character. Tell the story through their eyes to see how the story shifts or if the story shifts. This is not an exercise in trying to find reasoning for bad things, but to find perspectives that may be overlooked at first glance. Allow yourself to find the feelings that emerge in this practice. You might reach out to Aphrodite for wisdom or guidance or just healing for your own heart. After all, you cannot heal or change the hearts of others – but you can change your own.

Aphrodite doesn't ask you to forgive everyone. She asks you to heal your heart. That might mean confronting someone or removing someone from your life. Sit with Her and see what she has to say and what wisdom flows on the waters of Her being.

# Chapter 3

# Aphrodite Stories & Myths

*"Of all of the Twelve Olympians She is the most alarming and the most alluring, so much so that many writers have tended to edge away from a discussion of Her It is not that they write against Aphrodite, but rather that they avoid Her as a topic"* – "The Twelve Olympians" by Charles Theodore Seltman

When first researching Aphrodite, the experience can be fascinating. While there are references to Her in stories, it can almost seem as though She is relegated to a supporting or meddling role. Or it can seem as though She is highlighted in stories of love and affairs.

All of this is true, of course. But when you look at Aphrodite as someone with whom you might create a sacred relationship, the broader strokes She is often painted with become more defined the more you learn. Below, we will consider three of Aphrodite's stories.

## An Affair with Ares

What we need to remember is that Aphrodite was not pleased with being told to marry Hephaestus. She felt She was above him and that She could have better partners. And if we also remember that She was a virgin, as in one-in-herself, the lack of control in this decision was not something that settled well for Her.

She started a torrid affair with Ares, the God of War, while She was married. One night, when they were in each other's arms, the Sun God, Helius/Helios, saw them and told Hephaestus of this affair.

Hephaestus, being a crafty one, created an invisible net that was placed around the golden bed he had made for himself and Aphrodite. The net stretched all around the bed and to the wall. He told Aphrodite that he was going away for a while and laid the trap to catch Her and Ares.

Ares came for Aphrodite and lay on the bed with Her. And immediately the net captured them and held them down. They tried everything they could to free themselves from the bed, but there was no escape. While this was happening, Helios reported on what was happening to Hephaestus who came home – angry, but likely not surprised. Hephaestus called on the godds to come around and see what the two had done – and to shame them for their adulterousness. But Poseidon convinced Hephaestus to let them go, though Ares was then banished from the place of the godds for his actions.

## Psyche & Eros

Once upon a time, as many stories begin, there was a beautiful girl whose beauty rivaled all others, even Aphrodite. Psyche became known the world over for her mesmerizing looks and people came from faraway places to see her. Even with this attention, Psyche remained unmarried and her parents began to worry. Psyche's parents brought her to an oracle who, under the guidance of Apollo who was instructed by Eros to do so, told Psyche she was to marry a horrible beast.

Aphrodite had also asked Eros to poison mens' minds so they could not see the beauty of Psyche, as Aphrodite was not pleased with someone besides Her getting attention. However, what Aphrodite did not expect was Eros to fall in love with Psyche.

Psyche's parents were devastated by this news, but as it was the word of the godds, they went ahead and allowed their daughter to be married to the beast (Eros in disguise). As the story goes, Psyche was only able to be with her husband at night, according to the oracle, and he was a wonderful husband to her.

He was loving and kind, but Psyche was upset that she could only be with him at night, and she confided in her sisters her dismay.

Her sisters, being jealous of her partnership, talked Psyche into killing her husband as it was clear to them that he would harm and kill her eventually. Psyche went into her bedroom one night with an oil lamp and a knife with which to kill her husband. But as she held the lamp to his face, she saw the face of Eros, spilling the oil on his face.

Eros woke up and cried out that Psyche had betrayed him and her promise to never see her husband's face. He fled and Psyche followed him, trying to reunite with her love. In her searches, she was told to seek the counsel of Aphrodite – who had imprisoned Eros in a palace for his actions.

Aphrodite spoke to Psyche and gave her impossible tasks to achieve in order to be reunited with her love. All of these tasks filled Psyche with despair as she didn't know how she would accomplish them. And in all of the tasks, she returned to Aphrodite who became more and more angry that Psyche successfully accomplished the challenges.

There were seeds to sort, which were then carried by ants and sorted. Psyche then needed to gather a golden fleece from trampling rams, but got guidance by the water to wait until the sun went down and the rams were calmer. She was asked to gather water from the River Styx and got guidance and help from an eagle to collect the water. And finally, she was told to go to the underworld to get a box that contained an elixir of beauty, but she was warned by Aphrodite not to open the box. While this is a challenge Psyche does without worry, realizing she needs to give a cake to the three-headed dog to bypass that danger, she was curious, opened the box and fell asleep.

During all of these feats, Eros discovered what has happened and found a way to escape the palace to save Psyche. As a result of his love and her efforts, Zeus allowed them to be with each other and made Psyche immortal, allowing the two lovers to be together forever.

## The Judgment of Paris

There was a contest between the three most beautiful goddesses on Olympus: Aphrodite, Hera, and Athena. For whomever was deemed to be the most beautiful would receive a prize for being the fairest and that prize would be a golden apple.

At the wedding of Thetis and Peleus, all the godds had been invited – except for Eris, the goddess of discord. True to Her nature, Eris decided to come anyway and created the golden apple, causing all of the goddesses to speak out about who was the rightful recipient of the prize. There was so much disagreement that Zeus was called upon to help make the decision. But Zeus would not do it and called the goddesses to follow Hermes to Paris of Troy, the shepherd prince, to make the decision.

Aphrodite dressed herself in the finest of clothes, dyed in spring flowers, perfuming the cloth with the sweetest and most enticing of scents. Each of the goddesses spoke with Paris, trying to secure his affection and to secure the prize of the golden apple and the title of 'the fairest.'

Hera said that if Paris named her the fairest, she would make him the king of all men. Athena told Paris that she would make him victorious in war. Aphrodite in all of her cunning offered to Paris the hand of Helen. Because of this offering, Paris said that Aphrodite was the fairest of the three. But as history would unfold, the taking of Helen to be Paris' wife would lead directly to the Trojan War.

\* \* \*

Aphrodite's role in these stories is complex and yet convincingly human at times. She has desires that She wishes to fulfil, which might speak of Her power and might speak of Her selfishness.

Her marriage with Hephaestus is one of affairs and a husband who wants to keep Her in Her place.

As She becomes aware of Psyche, we see Aphrodite as manipulative of Eros and jealous of Psyche. But while these show a different side than the typical Goddess of Love label, they are also indicative of her ability to be affected by humans. After all, Psyche is not a god, but threatens the power of Aphrodite. In Her jealousy, we can also see Her as an initiator and challenger. She is the one who may be trying to stop Psyche or protect Eros. She might also be a godd who realizes that Psyche and Eros are meant to be together and wants to test the resolve of the relationship. In the end, Aphrodite does come to accept Psyche as Her son's wife.

In the story of the Golden Apple, we also see Aphrodite as the one who wants so badly to be seen as the fairest. Perhaps this is superficial or maybe it is a keen awareness of what makes Her revered. After all, if She has been known as the Goddess of Beauty, it would make sense for Her to want to hold onto that title. And it is clear She knows the heart of Paris is what needs to be swayed in order to get what She wants.

But there might be other ways to look at these stories. I hold these stories as being facets of a deity who has been put on a pedestal as something to look at versus a being with feelings and frailties. To me, this makes Her more approachable and more relatable. Not only can I see myself in the rashness of Her behaviors (at times), but I can also see a being whose heart wants to be safe and held.

# Chapter 4

# Aphrodite in the Present Time

When we look at Aphrodite worship in the modern time, there are varying interpretations of Her and how to worship Her. While there are some who prescribe reconstructing rituals based on the texts of the times, there are others who seek to find Aphrodite in the present time, where She shows up as a modern goddess who is shapeable and mutable (or at least open to interpretation).

I would offer that Aphrodite worship today does vary since personal relationships with Aphrodite are unique and often not out in public. There are many Witches, pagans, and magick practitioners who hold certain deities close and they have no need or desire to share their practices with anyone else.

There are others who do have rites that are public and dedicated only to Aphrodite and Her various facets. And there are also those who reenact Her festivals during the months of July and August every year as part of Hellenic Polytheistic Reconstructionism.

## Personal Practices

My experience tells me that many people work with Aphrodite because they have been called to Her. They don't necessarily have a personal experience, but they create a relationship based on that calling. They might, for example, read Her stories and sit with Her to get to know her better. And they might work with Her for a few moments and then walk away from practicing with Her.

There are a variety of books that contain specific rituals to Aphrodite, ones that have formed out of historical context and some from reconstruction and some from inspiration. If you're looking for specific, detailed scripts of rituals, I invite you to seek out Laurelei Black.

Since my work with Aphrodite is primarily a personal practice, I would also put into the mix the idea of working with Her from a purely inspirational space. I work with Her in the ways that seem most appropriate at the time. I don't necessarily follow scripts or liturgy or even an outline. Sometimes, it's just a matter of sitting down with Her to see what happens.

And sometimes, it's just as simple as allowing Her to inspire me over the course of a day. That magick is some of the most powerful – allowing myself to encounter the world through the eyes of a godd.

## Public Temples & Rituals

That said, I also help with public rituals as a ritualist and organizer. When we've planned rituals for Beltane, for example, we've chosen to call on Aphrodite as the deity for the entire ritual. While She is not someone the group is dedicated to and the members may not work with Her individually, She made it clear that She needed to be the central figure of that ritual. She was invoked and celebrated and gave Her blessing to the Maypole.

I am also aware of a group called Temple of Aphrodite, which holds gatherings in and around the Oakland, California area. They offer monthly opportunities to worship Her in person, with a rotating priestess/priestx group that takes responsibility for each ritual.

*"What are the ways that love has wounded your heart? Come to our temple and let Aphrodite be your guide as you mend the wounds of love.*

*The Temple of Aphrodite maintains a monthly liturgy & support space for those who wish to experience the mysteries of the goddess in Her many forms. We explore & celebrate the many ways love, beauty, desire & pleasure shape our decisions, choices, actions,* and lives. We recognize Aphrodite in the world around us today in Her contemporary guises with modern sensibilities." – via The Raven's Wing Magical Co.

There is also the Church of Aphrodite that was founded in 1938 by Gleb Botkin. This was founded on the idea that love is an energy that is timeless and not contained by the idea of a lifetime. This church was also founded on the premise that the world was birthed into being by a woman.

Some say this practice is more akin to Dianic Wicca, which focuses on the female as the center of ritual and magick. There is some modern discussion today around Dianic Wicca and its focus on defining women by their assigned gender at birth versus being accepting of those who transitioned to female or who seek to be seen as female/women.

*(In my own experience of Aphrodite, I find that She is accepting of all bodies, body histories, genders, gender histories, sexual histories, sexual natures, etc. so the idea of a practice that only acknowledges women seems limiting. Though I am certain She is quite happy with a practice that focuses on Her.)*

## Reconstructionism

At the simplest explanation, reconstructionism is a practice of trying to bring back the original rituals and intentions of those rituals into modern times. By researching old texts and various translations, Hellenic Reconstructionists seek to do things the way they were done in older times.

*"Hellenic polytheists worship the ancient Greek Gods, or the Hellenic pantheon, including the Olympians, nature divinities, underworld deities (chthonic gods) and heroes. Both physical and spiritual ancestors are honored. It is primarily a devotional or votive religion, based on the exchange of gifts (offerings) for*

*the gods' blessings. The ethical convictions of modern Hellenic polytheists are often inspired by ancient Greek virtues such as reciprocity, hospitality, self-control and moderation."* – Hellenism entry, Wikipedia

This practice allows for contact with the past to inform the modern practitioner. These rituals will often begin with cleansings, hymns, offerings or sacrifices, sharing of libations, and then prayers and a closing.

# Chapter 5

# Symbols, Offerings & Holidays

Personally, I'm not a subscriber to lists of things that you 'should' do for a deity. I feel that building a relationship is personal and you will create something that is uniquely between you and that godd.

And yet. It makes sense to begin somewhere. It makes sense to contemplate the stories others have told of Aphrodite and Her symbols and offerings. It makes sense to continue to revere Her at the days She has been celebrated for centuries. Begin where you might begin – and follow where She takes you next.

## Symbols & Offerings

Sky Chariot:

Aphrodite is said to have driven a two-yoked car of gold through the sky, according to the Orphic Hymn 55. Some describe this as being pulled by doves and others describe the chariot as one that in Her form as Venus, Vulcanus (Hephaestus) made Her as a wedding present. You can see images of this in the art of Aphrodite, as well as read about the chariot in Ovid's Metamorphoses.

Sea Chariot:

Though less referenced and possibly create for fictional pleasure, there are images of Aphrodite in a chariot related to the sea, one that was led by Triton.

Clothing & Jewelry:

In Homer's writings about Aphrodite, you will also find She is described as wearing white robes, an immortal robe woven by the Kharites, and pale white skin. In a translation of the

Homeric Hymn 6, She was born and immediately clothed in heavenly garments, a gold crown, and earrings in pierced ears with golden necklaces and jewels. Aphrodite is also described as wearing a glower crown made of crocus, hyacinth, violet, and rose, as well as lily and narcissus.

Magical Girdle:
The golden girdle that Aphrodite wears is one that enchants all that come upon it, as it is infused and empowered with love and desire. Some references speak of the girdle as being embroidered, while others describe the girdle as 'honeyed.' Most often, this girdle is associated with Aphrodite Philomeides (laughter or smile loving).

Palace:
In Greek epics, Aphrodite has a palace on Mount Olympus with Her consort, Hephaestus. Sometimes it's also called a bower or a tranquil place that's filled with cushions, where She lays Her head to rest.

Sacred Plants & Flowers:
Rose, Myrtle, Anemone, Myrrh, Apple, Lettuce, Pomegranate.

Animals:
Turtle Dove, Sparrow, Swallow, Swan, Shellfish, Fish, Hare, Swine.

Sacred Gems:
Pearl.

To make offerings to Aphrodite, you might create a space that is just for Her and just for things that She would like. This might be your altar, a place outside, a place by a body of water, etc. You might choose to leave a certain item consistently or adjust your offerings based on what She asks you to do.

You can also begin to connect other items, plants, and beings with Aphrodite as you cultivate your relationship with Her. She might very well reveal other offerings that would suit Her. Or you might offer things that relate to this list. Or you might do something completely different.

I will not tell you exactly what to do, but I will nudge you in the direction of things that are beautiful and sensual, things that fill you with delight in some way. As with any deity, make sure the offerings are fresh and replaced when they need to be replaced. You don't want to have Aphrodite's altar with a wilted rose, after all.

## Holidays & Celebrations

Aphrodite might appear to have been less of a major godd when looking back in time, but She continued to have festivals and holidays in Her name during the spring and summer months. People would gather to delight in Her energy, to bring offerings, and to ask the Goddess for Her blessings.

## Aphrodisia / Kinyrades

Celebrated in the spring for three days on the island of Cyprus, this festival included people from around the Mediterranean. People who attended would enjoy rich foods and sensual settings, while also engaging in competitive activities and a torch lit procession in the evening. There are some that place this in the month of July and within the month of Hekatombaion, around the third week of July to the third week of August.

While there are different descriptions of this ritual, there are some that seem to be consistent over time. The festival began with a cleansing, sometimes with the blood of a dove to sanctify the space and make an offering to Aphrodite. People would carry images of Her around the towns and process to be washed in preparation for being in Her presence. Those who were initiated into Her mysteries would also receive salt from the priests and bread shaped as phalluses in a reference to the story of Her birth.

Apart from the sacrifice of the dove, the offerings during this festival could not be bloody, so there would be offerings of incense, flowers, and fire. This festival was linked to Aphrodite Pandemos, or She of earthly, non-spiritual love.

Like Aphrodisia, Kinyrades was an involved ritual that included multiple days of preparation and celebration. Some describe this as having multiple levels of engagement, with the first being a payment of a coin to the priest who then offered salt in celebration of Aphrodite's birth.

As these are similar in description, they might be the same – some texts offer these two celebrations as two distinct celebrations.

In Kinyrades, there were sporting competitions followed by a day of cleansing in the sea and offering sacrifices to Her, which is familiar. From there, a devout one would need to stay up all night before being able to see the high priest.

Once accepted by the high priest, the next level would begin over the course of a few days, with ongoing lamentations of the death of Adonis. The devout would leave flowers and chant for him. To celebrated Adonis' resurrection, the songs turned to hymns and dancing followed.

In the end, the third level was a moment to honor the perfection of the ritual and its various rites.

\* \* \*

Other days/holidays that are attributed to Aphrodite in 'Cult of Aphrodite' by Laurelei Black include:

Fridays – Devotional work and meditation on Her

4th of each month – Offerings to Her

February 14 – Celebration of romantic and erotic love, Feast of Eros

April 1 – Peace, in commemoration of her subduing Ares

Fall Equinox – Mourning the loss of Adonis

There are also rites that Black notes as being related to moon cycles:

May's Dark Moon – Aphrodite is put to sea

3 Days after June's New Moon – A Mystery ritual and festival for Athena

October's Dark Moon – A time of mourning, madness, and release

Still others are mentioned by scholars and devotees of Aphrodite, as well as personal holidays of dedication, initiation, and connection. Some of these rites continue on today, though often with modern interpretations and offerings. As an example, I've been to a ritual to Aphrodite that included dancing to pre-recorded contemporary pop music around Her altar. While I'm certain some will argue that reconstructing rituals for Aphrodite is important, I would also point out that relationships with the godds, and the godds themselves, evolve over time. They evolve with context, time, and the needs of the people.

# Chapter 6

# Titles & Epithets

Aphrodite is known by many names, allowing Her to be known for Her various facets and qualities. For those who are seeking to get to know some part or parts of themselves, these names or titles or epithets allow for deepening into a more personal experience of Her. Some of Her epithets have been claimed because of translations of writings on Her, and some are disputed and argued in academic circles. But what I think is clear is that those who seek to know Her will find She arrives as She is meant to for that person. So, if you resonate with a particular title, you can work with that title in ritual, in song, in prayer, and in your heart.

This list has been compiled from a variety of sources and hymns, with special thanks to scholars and to those who would seek to know Her in all of Her parts. I have not found these accidentally. I have found these through research and various sources.

To help you better understand these titles, you might start each 'meaning' with the idea of 'She is' or 'She with' or 'She who':

Ælikovlǽpharos – (Elikoblepharus; Gr. ἑλικοβλέφαρος, ΕΛΙΚΟΒΛΕΦΑΡΟΣ) fluttering eyelids

Æratoplókamos – (eratoplocamus; Gr. ἐρατοπλόκαμος, ΕΡΑΤΟΠΛΟΚΑΜΟΣ) lovely locks of hair

Ærohtotróphos – (erototrophus; Gr. ἐρωτοτρόφος, ΕΡΩΤΟΤΡΟΦΟΣ) nurse or mother of love

Anadyomǽni – (anadyomene; Gr. ἀναδυομένη, ΑΝΑΔΥΟΜΕΝΗ) risen from the sea

Ánassa – (Gr. ἄνασσα, ΑΝΑΣΣΑ) queen

Aphroyǽneia – (aphrogenia; Gr. ἀφρογένεια, ΑΦΡΟΓΕΝΕΙΑ) foam-born

Éfkarpos – (eucarpos; Gr. εὔκαρπος, ΕΥΚΑΡΠΟΣ) fruitful.

Efpatǽreia – (eupatereia; Gr. εὐπατέρεια, ΕΥΠΑΤΕΡΕΙΑ. Noun.) daughter of a noble father

Efstǽphanos – (eustephanus; Gr. εὐστέφανος, ΕΥΣΤΕΦΑΝΟΣ) well-crowned or well-girdled

Kallípygos – (callipygos; Gr. καλλίπυγος, ΚΑΛΛΙΠΥΓΟΣ) beautiful buttocks (πυγή)

Kharidóhtis – (charidotes; Gr. χαριδώτης, ΧΑΡΙΔΩΤΙΣ. Noun.) giver of joy

Kleidoukhos – (cleiduchos; Gr. κλείδουχος, ΚΛΕΙΔΟΥΧΟΣ) She who holds the keys

Kourotróphos – (courotrophus; Gr. κουροτρόφος, ΚΟΥΡΟΤΡΟΦΟΣ) nurturer of children

Krýphios – (cryphius; Gr. κρύφιος, ΚΡΥΦΙΟΣ. fem./masc. nom. Adj.) hidden, concealed, occult, secretive

Kýpris – (Cypris; Gr. Κύπρις, ΚΥΠΡΙΣ) the place where She was born from the foam

Kyproyǽnǽs – (Cyprogenes; Gr. Κυπρογενὲς, ΚΥΠΡΟΓΕΝΕΣ) off the shores of Kýpros (Cyprus; Gr. Κύπρος) for, as told in the mythology, She emerged from the foam which formed when the genitals of Ouranós (Uranus; Gr. Οὐρανός) fell into the sea off the shore of the island

Lýkaina – (lucaina; Gr. λύκαινα, ΛΥΚΑΙΝΑ. Noun.) She-wolf

Mákaira – (macaera; Gr. μάκαιρα, ΜΑΚΑΙΡΑ) blessed

Ouranía – (Urania; Gr. Οὐρανία, ΟΥΡΑΝΙΑ) In Orphic hymn 55.1, Aphrodíti is called Ouranía, of the Sky, of Ouranós (Uranus; Gr. Οὐρανός) heavenly one

Pándimos – (pandemus, pandemia; Gr. Πάνδημος, ΠΑΝΔΗΜΟΣ) great power over the affections of all people; having dominion over the sexual unions of mortals; earthly, non-spiritual love

Peithóh – (peitho; Gr. πειθώ, ΠΕΙΘΩ. Proper name.) persuasion and seduction

Phílandros – (Gr. φίλανδρος, ΦΙΛΑΝΔΡΟΣ. Adj.) man-loving

Philommeidís – (philommeides; Gr. φιλομμειδής, ΦΙΛΟΜΜΕΙΔΗΣ. Adj.) laughter-loving or smile-loving

Philopánnykhos – (Gr. φιλοπάννυχος, ΦΙΛΟΠΑΝΝΥΧΟΣ. Adj. Etym. φιλο "friend" + πάννυχος "all night long.") friend of all-night festivity; religious festivals

Polyhymnus – See Polýÿmnos

Polytímitos – (polytimetus; Gr. πολυτίμητος, ΠΟΛΥΤΙΜΗΤΟΣ) highly honored

Polýÿmnos – (polyhymnus; Gr. πολύυμνος, ΠΟΛΥΥΜΝΟΣ. Adj. Pronounced: poh-LEE-eem-nohs) celebrated in many hymns

Potheinotáti – (potheinotate; Gr. ποθεινοτάτη, ΠΟΘΕΙΝΟΤΑΤΗ. Adj.) desirable

Pontogenes – See Pontoyænís

Pontoyænís – (pontogenes; Gr. ποντογενής, ΠΟΝΤΟΓΕΝΗΣ. Adj.) seaborn

Pótnia – (Gr. πότνια, ΠΟΤΝΙΑ. Noun.) mistress, queen

Sæmní – (semne; Gr. σεμνή, ΣΕΜΝΗ. σεμνός is masculine; σεμνή is feminine.) holy, exalted

Sceptuchus – See Skiptoukhos.

Skiptoukhos – (sceptuchus; Gr. σκηπτοῦχος, ΣΚΗΠΤΟΥΧΟΣ) bearing a scepter

Vasíleia – (Basileia; Gr. βασίλεια, ΒΑΣΙΛΕΙΑ) Queen

Viodóhtis – (biodotis; Gr. βιοδῶτις, ΒΙΟΔΩΤΙΣ) giver of life

Yænnodóteira – (gennodoteira; Gr. γεννοδότειρα, ΓΕΝΝΟΔΟΤΕΙΡΑ) giver of heirs

Yænǽteira – (geneteira; Gr. γενέτειρα, ΓΕΝΕΤΕΙΡΑ. Noun and adj.) birth-giver or mother

Zéfkteira – (zeukteira; Gr. ζεύκτειρα, ΖΕΥΚΤΕΙΡΑ. Noun. Fem. of ζευκτήρ.) causes mortals to propagate

(Source: http://www.hellenicgods.org/aphrodite-the-epith ets)

For those who want a simpler list:

Aligena (Sea Born)
Ambologera (She Who Postpones Old Age)
Anaduomene (Rising from the Sea)
Androphonos (Killer of Men)
Anosia (Unholy)
Apatouros (Deceptive One)
Apostrophia (She Who Turns Herself Away)
Areia (Warlike; of Ares)
Basilis (Queen)
Dôritis (Bountiful)
Eleemon (Merciful)
Enoplios (Bearing Weapons)
Epipontia (On the Sea)
Epistrophia (She Who Turns to Love)
Epitragidia (She Upon the Buck)
Epitumbidia (She Upon the Graves)
Euplois (Fair Sailing)
Euploia (Fair Voyage)
Genetullis (Genetrix)
Heteira (Courtesan)
Hera (of Hera; of Marriage)
Hôplismenê (Armed)
Kallipugos (of the Beautiful Buttocks)
Kallisti (the Fairest)
Kataskopia (Spying; Peeping)
Khruse (Golden)
Kupris (Cyprian)
Kuprogenes (Cyprus-born)
Kuthereia (Kytherean)

Limenia (of the Harbor)
Makhanitis (Deviser; Contriver)
Mechanitis (Skilled in Inventing)
Melainis (Black)
Migôntis (Marital Union)
Morpho (Shapely Form)
Nikêphoros (Bringer of Victory)
Nymphia (Bridal)
Ourania (Heavenly)
Pandemos (of All People)
Pasiphaessa (the Far-Shining)
Pelagia (of the Sea)
Philomeides (Laughter-Loving / Smile-Loving)
Porne (Fleshy; Prostitute)
Potnia (of the Sea)
Praxis (Action; Sexual)
Psithyristês (Whispering)
Skotia (Dark)
Suriê theos (Syrian Goddess)
Summakhia (Ally in War)
Symmakhia (Ally in Love)
Tumborukhos (Gravedigger)
Xenia (of the Foreigner)
(Source: Theoi.com)

## Working with Titles

I have found that Aphrodite is sometimes put into the world as a love goddess, which is true, but not complete. Instead, one might look at Her as a goddess who arrives in the way that She arrives for a person. She offers a wide array of qualities and stories to bring one's heart closer to joy and comfort.

If you are called to work with Her titles, you might find that one is calling to you at this moment. You may find that different names will call to you at different moments, while some never will. When you are working with Her, you may find you come to Her in Her qualities and then become more discerning by using Her titles. Do as you will.

Some ways I've found helpful in working with Her titles are:

**Deep exploration** – While I don't purport myself to be an academic, I do find that meeting a godd requires you to be inquisitive. You may want to find a title that sings to you and use the resources you have to look into it. What does it mean in Greek? How is it used? Where did it show up in Aphrodite's hymns and stories? What did it mean in the context it was found? What does it mean in the context of today and of your life?

**Spellwork** – I recommend using Her titles in your spellwork, whatever that means to you. You might use one of Her titles as a way to meditate on a quality of your life or a quality you want to cultivate in your life. You may also want to bring Her titles into invocations, or callings, to Her. You can also bring Her titles into spells you might create, calling upon a facet to aid you in your personal work.

**Altars** – Placing pictures or offerings to the epithet of Aphrodite that most calls to you can help to focus your intention. You might bring sea water to the names of sea foam birth or you might lay down precious items for the queen or you might place a picture of yourself smiling to bring the smile-loving Aphrodite into your mind.

**Chants and songs** – You can also use Aphrodite's titles to chant and sing to Her, or to chant and sing to yourself. Repeating a name again and again to yourself can move you into an altered state where you can become closer to Her presence. You might also want to have some names in your mind to call upon certain qualities you need in certain situations. For example, when I want to focus on the daily work of my life, I might call on Aphrodite Praxis to take action.

While I move toward and away from Her titles, I know Aphrodite to be as complicated as She is wondrous. With these various interpretations of Her being, I know Her to be as complex as my own experience. I can feel more connected and more alive in worship of Her.

## Chapter 7

# Chants & Altar Ideas

I confess that my personal practice of magick offers permission for spontaneity and the birth of chants with little preparation or planning. I am at ease when I can simply pull myself into a state of connection and then move from there to bliss. But that isn't a helpful statement for those seeking to move closer to a specific practice.

What I will say about singing to Aphrodite or chanting is that remembering Her love is a way into the mystery of this creation. Knowing Her and knowing myself is another way into letting go of expectation of outcome.

### Bringing Chants into Practice

When the memory of Her birth on sea foam glides into my mind, I know Her to be birthing and arising. From this place, I can offer gratitude and reverence. From a place of true exploration, it becomes less of how to make something happen and more of allowing something to emerge.

If you are seeking to create a chant for Aphrodite, think on the ways that you already encounter and experience Her. Think on the things you want to ask Her or the things you want to emulate in Her. Perhaps it is love. Perhaps it is sexual desire. Perhaps it is joy. Perhaps it is something different.

Bring yourself into a state of connection with the feeling that you want to explore. I invite the possibility that you can do this simply by showing up as you are. You can step into the expanse of desire to create and thus become a creator.

Things You Need:
Time and privacy

Paper

A writing instrument you enjoy holding

A recording device (if you have access to such a device and
want a recording to come back to the song/chant at a later
time)

To begin, bring out a piece of paper and allow yourself ten
minutes to write down everything you want to see happen in the
chant or song. What do you want to say? What do you want to
invoke? What do you want to feel?

Let it all out on the page, even if you're not sure it's right or
proper in this moment. Just let everything out to play on the
paper. You may want to write small or large or you might find
you come back to the same word again and again.

If you're stuck on what to say, write out a word and then
write out all the words that you relate to this word. Write out
images and feelings and experiences. Capture what you can
with the realization that your work is between you and Her.

Once you have all the words on the paper, take a breath. Thank
yourself for your action. Thank yourself for your vulnerability.
Close your eyes and think about Her. Call into your mind what
you think She looks like, whether this is the vision of Her in a
seashell or the one who luxuriates in some beautiful place. Bring
Her into your mind as best you can, with all the qualities you
know of and those that still seem right to you.

When Her energy has filled you and started to electrify your
skin and bones, take a moment to ask Her for guidance. Ask Her
for how you need to know Her and how you to need to celebrate
Her at this time.

The moment you feel you have Her within you and the
moment you feel Her guiding you, open your eyes again and
read the words that you have on the paper. Soften your gaze
and find the words that are calling to your attention first. Circle
those. You may find that you only circle a few words. You might

circle more than a few words. You may find you circle groups of words. Once you feel done with this point, begin to write the words you circled on a new piece of paper. Find out what you have brought into awareness. Can you make sentences out of these? Can you create a poem that rhymes?

Or maybe you find the words are able to come together in a chant that doesn't need fillers or polishing. What do you see? What is the gift that She gave you and that you are giving back to Her? Some find that they can settle here and stop with the chant writing process. Others might begin to feel a tune in their minds and try to sing different things until the song feels complete. This is why it can be helpful to have a recording device. It can help you try out new things until you find something that you like – and then remember it when you're done.

You can continue in this space for as long as you like. You might turn your time with Aphrodite into a ritual or a spellworking or a quiet time of reflection. You might simply bask in the beauty of Her willingness to create with you. Or you might find that you create a song or chant, thank Her, and then stop what you are doing for the moment.

You can stay in the trance-like state for as long as you like. I only suggest that you find a way to bring things to a close by putting the paper away and having something to snack on at the end to ground yourself.

## Songs for Ritual

While it's easy to find songs about the ocean online, it's less common to find songs about Aphrodite. They exist, but those from the heart tend to be more personal and magickally powerful.

One of my favorite songs to use in working with Aphrodite is by Starhawk.

### The Ocean is the Beginning of the Earth - Starhawk
The ocean is the beginning of the Earth

The ocean is the beginning of the Earth
All life comes from the sea
All life comes from the sea

I have also written a few chants that are easily used in Aphrodite workings. While they have tunes, you are welcome to use these as you like and find the song that sings to you.

**Down to the Sea (2016) - Irisanya**
Down to the sea, we gather
Making ready our hearts
Down to the sea, together
Making ready our hearts
We gather, we gather
Sacred, solemn, and true
We gather, we gather
Sacred, solemn, and true

**Aphrodite (2015) - Irisanya**
Your heart knows the way
Stepping into the sea
Dropping all apologies
Magickal and free

## The Aphrodite Altar

One of the things I learned early on about Aphrodite is that a goddess of beauty loves to have beautiful things to celebrate Her. One of the other things I learned is that She is more than happy to have multiple altars in every corner of a home, so it can be good to make the altar space you do have available as generous as possible.

I have some personal thoughts about what an Aphrodite altar should include, and I have adjusted my own practices over time. You will find what works best for you, of course, and here are some starting points that can help:

Seashells
Roses (preferably) / Flowers
Pearls
Images / Statues
Mirrors
Oils – rose, in particular
Honey
Greek foods and beverages
Chocolate
Apples

I have also added in stones that are rose colored or heart healing, e.g. rose quartz, rhodochrosite, etc.

I begin with a space that is large enough for the offerings I want to have for Her. I clean the space with water and remove any dust from Her space. Remember, this is a place where Her energy and presence will live, so it is vital to make a home that is welcoming.

I will often put down an altar cloth of pink or red or white. To me, this brings in Her sweetness and Her sensuality. The cloths will have a smooth or velvety texture, again, adding the energy that beauty is an experience, not just an image.

I place a picture or statue of Aphrodite in the center and put lovely things and offerings around Her. I have noticed She is a deity who is quite content to have multiple images of Herself around, so if you have other images of Her, arrange them as you like. My personal practice includes necklaces of pearls around the base of Her feet, as well as silky scarves.

The creation of an altar is a personal practice, to be sure. Your relationship with Aphrodite may be one that suggests other items. I also have olive branches around Her, as well as a bottle of water from Delphi to help Her feel more at home.

For those who don't have a lot of space for altars or who need to keep their altars private or hidden, you can also have small offerings to Her. A shell on your desk or bedside table can be an altar. A mirror that you write Her name on can be an altar. A small bowl of ocean water can be an altar to Her.

While having an altar is part of relationship building and setting the table for connection with a deity, it is also a place you should visit and spend time to continue to cultivate relationship. Take time to visit your altar every day. It doesn't have to be long. It doesn't have to be complicated. But visit the altar, return, show up, and be present. Make sure the altar stays clean, that the offerings (if you've left any) stay fresh, and that you move things as they feel they need to be moved.

## Blessing your Aphrodite Altar

When your altar is complete and ready, you might want to bless it by finding offerings to bring to Her. I often light some rose incense and light a candle on the altar that is only for my time with Her. You can take some salt water and sprinkle it around the altar as a cleansing and opening.

Welcome Her into your home or wherever your altar might be. Welcome Her, thank Her for coming and being present. This is also a time when you might make promises to Her about how you will tend Her Altar and how you will show up for Her.

You can make vows about being committed to Her. You could combine this with a dedication ritual or you could simply greet Her. And you can also talk to Her about why you have put things on the altar for Her. You can tell Her about why you are asking for Her presence.

While it can be expensive, a special rose oil can be a wonderful way to bless your altar. Or even taking some rose petals and rubbing them over the altar can be another way to seal in the promise of relationship with Her.

# Chapter 8

# Working with the Aspects of Aphrodite

When you first hear the name Aphrodite, you may have different images that come to mind. More often than not, you will find She is spoken of as the Goddess of Love and Beauty. While this is part of the story, I also feel it is limiting – and sometimes off putting as a first impression.

Just like any being, godd or not, She is complicated. And just as with any relationship, the more you get to know someone, the more complicated they become, the more you get to know Aphrodite, the more you see.

You begin to see the ways in which being a Goddess of Love means more than wanting everyone to be in love. It's that too, but it also means She wants to bring people together because SHE thinks they should be in love.

Or She becomes jealous of those thought to be more beautiful than She. Or She sets up challenges to try to trick or hurt another.

She doesn't just sit on a seashell. She shows up in myth and story and song. She shows up as the one who makes things happen, and also as the one who has a number of lovers.

> She shows up for those who call to Her – whether intentional or not.
> She shows up in the moments of love and longing for love.
> She shows up for those encountering questions of fertility and creation.
> She shows up for those seeking to know pleasure and beauty.
> She shows up in times of confusion and despair.
> She shows up in times of initiation – wanted and not.

What becomes clear is that the relationship you have with

Aphrodite – or that She might have with you – can be informed by the aspect of Her that is most compelling. One moment you might be drawn to the way She interacts with love and another day you might find Her rage to be the place that you know.

In all of these aspects, there are ways to explore the energies of this divine being and further know yourself. Perhaps you want healing or knowledge or understanding or just to know you're not alone. All of that is possible with Her.

## Love

If your heart is aching with fullness or emptiness, you can call on Aphrodite. She offers soothing and calm to the weary and the wanting, and She offers celebration to the lover and the loved.

For some, Aphrodite is the goddess that offers a hand into the places of love that stretch beyond romantic partnerships. She is the goddess that sings the song of coming to know what love is for you.

## Bringing in Love

I want to tell you that Aphrodite is a love spell. She is the intention of bringing forth that which is your birthright – to know yourself as love and in love.

Things you need:
1 rose
1 white tea light candle
White bowl, half filled with water

Begin by creating a space that is safe and sacred to you. You might find a shower or ritual bath might be a good place to begin, or you might feel ready without any preparation. You may choose to be naked or to wear minimal clothes, as you like.

Find yourself breathing the way that you do, without trying to change it or fix it. Find yourself in the way that you are in the moment, perfect and beautiful – however this looks or feels to you.

Allow your mind to begin to create a feeling of love in your body. This might be the kind of love that is shared between partners or it might be love that is larger than the universe, undefinable and vast. Whatever love you want to bring into your life, allow it to fill the places of your heart, your mind, your mouth, your hands, your feet, and even the spaces between all of those stretches of skin. When you feel this love in your body, allow this to fill your consciousness and push away anything that does not serve what you want to invite.

When you feel this love resonate in your body, and you will know exactly when, take the white candle and light it, placing it beside the bowl. Hold the rose in your hands. Begin to watch the light reflect in the water, and allow your eyes to soften until you can see beyond the water and into its fluidity. Sink your awareness into the water and begin to feel the petals of the rose, their shape and their texture.

Notice the smell of the rose as it floats around the room and bring it to your nose as you continue to deepen into the watery bowl. Begin a spell of love that drops into the water with each petal you remove and place into the bowl.

I am love.
I am worthy of love.
I invite love.
I am love.
I receive love.
I feel love.
I am love.

You are infusing the bowl with love and with the blessing of Aphrodite. Continue to repeat the words that feel the strongest to you, continuing to drop petals into the water and allowing your focus to be soft and gentle.

When the words begin to fall away and you feel as soft as a rose petal, take your hands and dunk them into the water. Begin to wash your face and heart and body with the water before you. Allow your intentions that sank and swam in the water to become a part of you. They might cleanse you of old stories, they might simply bring the shine of love's radiance to your skin. You might rub the rose petals over the places that ache or the heart that was broken.

In this moment, do what feels right to prepare yourself for love. To ready yourself. Sit with the way you feel. Allow the candle to burn out on its own time.

Take the rose petals and place them under your pillow. Leave one for Aphrodite. Rest deeply in your love.

## Knowing Self Love

While it seems obvious now, I was surprised by the self-love lessons from Aphrodite. I had been caught up in a love that reached outward instead of inward.

Things you need:
A clean bathtub
A large mirror
Eyeliner or marker or body paint or paint
Bathtub
Epsom salt
Sugar
Honey

Begin to fill a bathtub with warm water and some Epsom salt, as much as you like, though a cup is a good amount. As the bath is filling, remove your clothing and stand in front of a mirror. It might be helpful to have the lights on or off, depending on the time of day. You might choose to have a candle to light the darkness. Let whatever you choose to be perfectly you.

Take a few deep breaths and look at your reflection. Look over the places that have changed over time. Look at the scars and the shapes and the way your arms move when you lift them. Move around, know your body and begin to point out the things you love.

I love my elbows.
I love my collarbone.
I love my eyes.

And once you have loved all of the parts of your body that come easily, move to the other parts that need more attention – more LOVING attention.

I love my thighs.
I love the lines by my mouth.
I love the scar that I always cover up.
I love the shape of my _____.

Allow your body to know your love, welling from within, even in the moments where it might sound forced. Your body believes what you tell it. Aphrodite wants you to love all of the parts of yourself that are hidden, whether from your own hiding or from the messages of the overculture.

I love my _____.

Take the paint or the eyeliner or the marker and write 'I love you' all over your body. Write it on the places that need your love and the places that know your love. Draw hearts and stars and other symbols with meaning for you. Write out love letters that stretch from your fingers to your shoulders. Write poems on your thighs and your sex. Write of deliciousness and pleasure.

Write of the things you always wanted to say and know. If you are getting to know your body or seeing your body in new ways, allow this exercise to be an introduction – a first date. Perhaps the first of many.

If you find this to be a challenge, start with your hand. If you need, start with a foot. You can start with any place that feels good (and safe) and let the love find its way to new places. Ask Aphrodite to tell you how to get there, how to travel, how to know. Once you are done, look at yourself in the mirror and see what a piece of art you are. Touch the places that are loved and that are love.

Sink into the bathtub and begin to soak in the love messages so they might travel to places you could not reach – or the ones you could not touch just yet. (Again, if you want a smaller step, wash just the part of your body that you are focusing on in this moment.) Soak in the love of yourself and the knowing that you can actively love yourself. Engage this, know this, become this. Close your eyes and feel loved. Loved without another having to say a word. Loved without needing to feel a certain way. Feel the way love feels to you. All over your body.

Once the bath has cleared away the writing (and even if it hasn't), stand up and allow the water to flow out of the tub into the drain. Born of water, like Aphrodite, become born and alive in your own love. And if you still don't quite feel the rinsing away of anything that might not be yours to hold onto, you can use a mixture of sugar and honey to scrub the messages of love into your body, smoothing away any rough edges and any hesitant areas that still need tending to.

Don't scrub away the love; smooth it and shine yourself like a jewel.

## Fertility & Procreation

(Note: I am a white, cis-gendered female, but I am going to use language that I hope can be inclusive for all genders, gender histories, *and internal/external experiences.)*

"To assign 'fertility' as the singular meaning of a Goddess is possible only in the sense of a concept which recognizes woman merely as a function, but not as essential being," – 'Goddesses of Sun and Moon' by Karl Kerenyi

One of the potential challenges to relationship with Aphrodite could be the way She is related to fertility and procreation. This comes from a history of interpretations by men that often wanted things to be binary and heterosexual in presentation. I want to challenge this by offering broader definitions of fertility and procreation, knowing that many bodies can give birth and that many bodies may not be able to give birth.

Let us hold fertility more loosely, and yet widely. Let us hold this as creation, in all of its forms. As we see Aphrodite calling love to beings, we too can call love to the parts of ourselves that birth beauty in other forms.

You can adjust the Self Love exercise to be more suitable for a body that is giving birth soon, wrapping the growing child with words of love and health. Or you could write on your body of the desire for a child. In working with Aphrodite and Her energies of fertility, we can turn to the plant world and the metaphor of growth.

Things you need:
Seeds and soil or a baby plant
Container
Decorating materials

Find yourself in a place of quiet where you will not be interrupted. Pull into yourself the image of what you want to grow and create. Be detailed, be clear, take the time you need to know all of its sensations and intricacies. Let the feeling of what it is becoming the only thing you can think of in the moment. Know who is there, what you are wearing, what you are doing, and what you are feeling when the 'thing' happens. Be daring, have pride, know you deserve this thing, big or small.

When you feel full on the feeling, and not a second before, begin to decorate the pot with images that remind you of what you want and what you are growing. You might use words, you might use symbols, you might use pictures. You might simply sing to the soil or caress the seeds or plant leaves. Tell the container all of your desires. Tell it why you want to create it.

You can also bring your personal fluids into the pot, e.g. your spit, your blood, etc. Rub them on the pot to bring yourself into this act of creation and know yourself as a co-conspirator of creation. Once the pot is ready, raise it above your head and say something sweet to Aphrodite.

> Sweet one, dear one, beloved
> May your blessings splash around me
> May your hands wrap around mine
> May your heart wrap around my greatest desire
> Sweet one, dear one, beloved
> Aphrodite

Plant the seed or seeds. Plant the plant in the container. Make ready the vessel of creation and tend to it. Talk to it, remind it of what you want. Allow it to grow into your life alongside what you have called in. And if the seeds do not grow or the plant withers, you can always start again. There is no failure in attempting to grow and to emerge from the depths.

## Pleasure & Beauty

One of the natural entry points into work with Aphrodite is around beauty and sensuality. She is the golden one, the curved one, She who arises on sea foam, and She who seeks to spread love across the world. If you are feeling as though you need more love, more self-love, more intimacy with the person you are in this moment, Aphrodite is your being. And even if you want to work with Her peripherally, versus a long-term relationship, I find She is open to that sort of connection too. For those who want to bring pleasure into their lives, you might take various approaches.

## Immerse Your Senses

In a world that keeps us busy (thanks capitalism) and distracted, it can be difficult to remember the senses we have. Certainly, they allow us to know when something is wrong or when something has shifted, but they are less engaged in the radical act of noticing and luxuriating in the experience of a moment (or two). The world is rich with experience and with the possibility of wonder, of awe, but only when we stop to take a look.

I invite you to find a place that feels out of your ordinary experience. This might be a museum, a library, a park, or some other place near your home. Give yourself time to be in this place and to feel all of the sensations that come into your consciousness. Look around to see what you see. Close your eyes to feel the way the space feels. Touch what you can touch to see what is smooth and rough and surprising. Listen for the expected noises and the sounds you didn't notice when you weren't paying attention.

If there is a way to taste, dive into that sensation. If there isn't, stick out your tongue to taste the air or the way the water floats along the next breeze. Smell the way things are from room to room and place to place. What changes? What stays the same?

I invite the possibility that while you might focus on one sense at a time, you can also hold all of these senses at once. Give yourself the permission to be overwhelmed and inundated with information and experience. And breathe into this. You might even want to take a breath and hold it in, as you might hold this knowledge that you can be completely in all of your senses – whenever you want to be. You can be the person who is constantly filled with the understanding of beauty and presence.

While you might need a few introductions to this way of being, you can also expand this exercise into the 'everyday' world. What would it be like to engage all of your senses at home? At work? At a religious gathering? When you're playing with children or talking with friends?

What if you could be enraptured by the beauty of the world and all of its experiences – all the time?

## Beauty Immersion & Reflection

When you've cultivated your senses and you've brought them into more of your awareness, you can begin to take them out to play. I notice I can walk more easily with Aphrodite in the 'outside world,' when you look at the world through the lens of beauty. If I can turn off my cynicism for a moment (or more), I can begin to see the everyday beauty in the world. I can turn my attention and intention to the places that allow me to feel free and hopeful.

If I can bring my mind to beauty, I can be the person I want to be in the world. After all, when I know beauty, I remember what is important. When I know beauty, I maintain hope and energy to continue to fight for, work for, and strive for more. When I take away beauty from my life, just as when I take away healthy foods or sleep, I get tired more easily. I stop doing the things that need to be done. I need to refill on beauty. Every day. With your senses engaged, you can turn the dial to beauty.

Where do I find beauty? Where can I witness beauty? How can I know its name and its flavor? What about that tree or that rock? What about the way that piece of paper is folded in the wastebasket? Stop. Look. See.

How is this beautiful too? How is this part of the beauty of life? How is this allowing me to remember the sensual nature of my own being? How can this remind me that even when I forget beauty, I still am beauty? Am I beauty too?

Take time to walk around your world in all of its complexities and possibilities. Allow this to be the time it needs to be or the time that you have available. But make time. Make time to allow for moving past boredom and trying to get it 'right.' Turn off your phone. Forget what you were doing before or after. Just be in that moment and the one after that.

Some find it helpful to write down what they saw and what they experienced as a record of what could happen the next time. It can also help to collect beauty so that you can refer back to it when it's not as present in your life – during those hard times, the ugly times. Others might find it helpful to make a list of the things that were beautiful and surprisingly so. Or to make a list of the things that evoke the most pleasure. Do those change or do they become anchors into the experience of beauty?

If possible, walk with and in beauty daily. Make it a personal practice to open up and be aware. You don't have to spend forever in these moments, just enough time to allow the experiences to seep into your bones – and remain a part of you.

## Date Yourself

The greatest gift that Aphrodite has given to me is the permission to love myself. I tried finding it in other deities, other practices, and other places, but it finally settled into my heart when I met Her. She very clearly told me to have more fun and to worry less.

She also encouraged me to take myself on dates, much as Julia Cameron suggests for writers and creatives. The very thought of dating myself was a new concept and one that rattled against my internalized feelings of not being worth the time or effort. (To be fair, I've never been someone who dated folks. I was either in a relationship or I wasn't.)

I started out slowly, finding times where I would focus on doing things that I wanted to do, on the schedule that I wanted to follow. I stopped listening to the needs of everyone else or the ways that I could support their desires and listened to my own.

It was quiet for a while. It was still for a while. When you haven't been taking care of yourself or focusing on yourself in any way, you forget. You forget what is important to you. You don't know what it is to have fun or what makes you happy. At least, that was my experience. It was frustrating and it left me in a place of grief for the moments I didn't take for myself. But then I started dating myself, wooing myself, and allowing myself to feel the love from within.

I began with time to myself. Then I tried out a few things to see if I liked them. After all, I was out of practice, so it was likely that I wasn't going to get it right at first. I started to take more time for myself. The times became less about 'making' myself do things, and more about really enjoying this space. I began to smile more and laugh more. I started knowing how to speak up for myself in relationships because I knew what I wanted. And while there are times when I forget or when I step back from the focus on myself, when I return, I know She is smiling.

To extend the power of this practice of dating yourself, I encourage you to try writing about the date afterward. Write about what you liked, what you didn't like, and what you will remember about the time. You might talk about yourself in the third person: "I really liked it when Irisanya took me to…" or you might want to write about the date as though you were writing to a best friend or to the diary.

Write as though no one else is going to read the entries. Write honestly about what you love and what you don't. Write about the relationship with yourself that will always be there, even in its rough patches, and find the way home to a place that is joyful, pleasurable, and true.

## Troublemaker

When it comes to Aphrodite, it can be easy to focus on the beauty and the love and the wonder that She brings. But She's also a troublemaker who tries to bring people together and She's also a person who wants what She wants – and She'll do whatever it takes.

Perhaps you're in a place in your life where you feel you haven't caused enough trouble – or in a place where you feel that you could stand to reevaluate your intentions. She can help with that too.

## Making Trouble

You might experience yourself as a person who doesn't speak up for what you want in your life.

You might experience yourself as a person who has trouble pointing out problems or saying your truth in a moment where it might be challenging. You might also relate to yourself in this time as a person who is unsure that what they want is what they should have.

If this sounds like you or you've experienced this, let's turn to our lady, Aphrodite. She of gossamer hair and laughter, She who meddles in the affairs of others. While She might not always get the outcomes She wants – nor do the people who are part of Her plan, She moves forward with confidence and courage. She says what She says, does what She does, and makes sure Her wishes are known.

You may have been told a story at some point that you don't get what you want in life. You can't say everything that's on your mind. You can't possibly know what's good for others. No matter which (or all or another) of these stories resonates with you, it's time to let go of the stories and step into your power. The right time is right now.

Step into the center of you own life, of your own choices. You can do this by finding out what's important to you. This might take the form of a list, of a piece of art, of a set of pictures, or a song that jumps into your head. What do you want to be important in your life? What are your values, your priorities, and your truths? What things do you want to bring to the forefront of your life (that you maybe haven't at this point)?

I invite you to take this process into a sacred space of some kind. If you have access to a private place, find that. Before you begin, take some water, add sea salt, and stir that water around in a bowl. Let the water become blessed with the possibility of identifying what you want. Let the bowl be blessed with the knowledge you already have inside of you.

You might choose to wash your hands before you begin to write. Or you might find the water needs to just be there to collect any hesitation or fear that comes up as you write. Give yourself the space to write out the things that are important to you, that you want to speak up for. And once you have those on a piece of paper, find a new piece of paper and write them out again. You might use special paper for this or you might decorate the paper to help bring power to these powers of yours.

Take that piece of paper and put it in a place where you will read it every single day. For many, this is the bathroom or a bedroom. Allow yourself space each day to bring yourself back to yourself. You don't need to be perfect or to speak up for what you want EVERY day, but the more you bring these values into your present mind, the more likely they are to become what you do – versus what you want to do in your life.

When you take care of yourself, when you speak up, and when you live in your truth (no matter how small the gesture seems), take a moment to let Aphrodite know. She delights in the way that humans bring themselves back to their hearts.

## Making Up for Trouble

To be clear, I'm a firm believer that some trouble is needed in this world. I think the more we believe ourselves to be separate, the more difficult it becomes to remember we're not alone in the world.

That said, you may also come to Aphrodite with experiences

that have resulted in trouble for others. You may have meant well, but when things go badly (again and again), it might be a sign you need to look at yourself.

A wise way to look at the way you're showing up is to find a trusted friend who will tell you the truth in a gentle way. Ask them if there are patterns they have noticed that might be damaging. Ask them if they've been the victim of intentions gone awry. This is not an exercise in criticism. This is an invitation into forgiveness.

We all make mistakes – big and small. We all take chances and hurt others. We all have times when we really think we're doing the right thing. And we don't know of another way – until we find out we chose the wrong one. Step back from the mistake/misstep. It is not you. It is only something that happened.

In fact, write it down or put its energy into an item that you can place on the floor in front of you. Take a moment to walk around this paper or this item to get a look at the different sides. You might look at each side as a person who was involved. What did things look like from that angle? You might look at the different sides of the impacts and outcomes. What happened? What might have happened? What happens next?

Once you have looked around and looked at the sides, even if you're not clear what the sides might be, step as far back as you can from the item or paper to feel into the separation that exists now. If we can only make changes in this moment, then we need to step away from the past and the future. Take actual steps way. Until the item or paper becomes a speck in the distance.

If you don't have a lot of space to do this, then take the item and burn it or break it. Let it go. Let the attachment go. Let the moment go. But the best magick here is forgiveness. Even if you can't get forgiveness from someone else – or you don't want to ask – you can give yourself the gift of forgiveness. You can tell yourself that it's okay, that you're okay, and that things will pass.

This is a great place for mirror work, for telling yourself in the mirror that you forgive yourself. You soothe yourself by saying it's okay and that you had good reasons for things to be the way they were. And then you can repeat that you forgive yourself. Continue to say those words until they lose meaning or they don't sound like words anymore. And when this point happens, let yourself be surrounded by the love of Aphrodite. Allow yourself to feel Her arms or to sink into a shell or to simply know Her presence to be the way to seal this spell of forgiveness.

When you find yourself back at the memory of the thing that went wrong, remind yourself that you have forgiven yourself. You can let it go and you can move away from that person you used to be. Turn to Aphrodite not only as a caring being, but also as a being who has gotten Herself into some not-so-great situations, and She still moved on – She still did what She thought was best.

## Challenger

While I was brought to Aphrodite for the love and the beauty bits, I stayed in my relationship with Her because of the way She is the Initiator. She challenges Psyche to various feats, for example, and while the story is often told in the negative impacts on Psyche, we can also look at this story as an initiation story.

To see Her as a challenger begins with seeing the ways in which we ask to be changed. One of the main elements of an initiation is the deep call from within to move from one place to another, from one state of being to another.

It is true that initiations are sometimes called for by us and sometimes thrust upon us for no apparent reason. They are journeys of revealing. They are steps toward something that is unknown. They are opportunities to take away all that is known and replace it with what is becoming.

Aphrodite does ask the question: are you in contact with your sensual self? Are you in contact with the beauty you are? Are you experiencing pleasure? Are you?

Aphrodite asks us core shifting questions. For if we are to take on pleasure, we have to look at how we hold ourselves back. If we are to invite in beauty, we need to recognize how we have dismissed the beauty of our being. And perhaps as you start to touch into these questions, you realize that you are actually the initiator. You are the challenger and the challenges. There's work to do.

## Self-Dedication with Aphrodite

I personally have found that when I sign up for initiatory journeys, they are less likely to completely surprise me. When I am the one who says, "Yes, I'm ready to find out what I can become," I am more in control and I am less afraid of what happens. (Of course, this doesn't mean things are easy or even fun. It does mean that I signed up for what is coming. All of it.)

There are witchcraft traditions that offer initiation rites and journeys. There are steps you can take, things you can study, and vows you can make. But what you need to know as a witch or a magick maker or priestess or priestx is that you are the one who can make choices for yourself.

If you want to do a self-dedication or initiation, you are well within your power to do it. Some will disagree, but I want you to do what's right for you. I hold dedication to be a blessing of the work that you will do with a certain deity or aspect, while initiation is more about challenging your internal structures to see how they might change or shift your external reality. I also hold initiation to be a place where there is a receiving of power or energetic connection to a larger tradition, practice, deity, etc.

If you feel the call to dedicate yourself to Aphrodite, I suggest you spent at least one moon cycle with Her to see if you're a good fit. You can talk with Her, journal to Her, and see what emerges in that month. If you're still feeling that things are heading in the direction of lady love, you might set aside a time to dedicate yourself to Her.

First things first, I recommend dedicating yourself for a year and a day. This allows there to be a full exploration, but also a point of checking in to see if things are still working. You may find that working with Her for a year and a day is enough, thank you very much. You may find you want to add on more time or maybe do something more formal for dedication.

It's all up to you. And even more importantly, you need to remember that Aphrodite should be in the conversation too. You should listen to see what messages She has for you, what signs She might offer in your direction. Does Aphrodite tell you She loves apples or strawberries? Does She say you need to go to the water on Fridays? Listen. And when you have heard Her and you have listened to yourself, you can begin to craft a ritual. Here are some pieces you might include:

Cleanse your body
Create sacred space (grounding, casting/elements, invocation
    to Aphrodite)
Sit in a meditative space with Her
Tell Her your vows and promises and goals
Feel into Her presence and Her connection to you
Anoint yourself with salt water or a rose oil, perhaps in a
    heart shape
Thank the energies you called in and open the circle

You can do this outside, by the water, or in your bedroom. You can be elaborate with what you wear and what you do, or you can be simple.

What is important in these initiatory rites and promises is that you are truthful about what you want and what you will do in return. You are making a commitment to showing up to do the work that you are tasked to do. And it will not all be easy or fun or even make sense. Show up anyway.

You might want to spend a month working through different

aspects of Aphrodite, learning about Her symbols and epithets, reading them and surrounding yourself with images of Her. Another month you might spend time writing songs and poems to Her. You might simply stand in a rose garden and say Her name.

You might learn some Greek phrases or you might take time to challenge the obstacles to loving yourself. You might sit in reflection with Her, by a simple altar, and tell Her about the struggles you're facing. Ask Her what you should do. Listen. Follow the waves where they take you. Return to Her. Return to yourself.

Think of self-dedication and self-initiation as a place of beginning to enter the liminal space of knowledge. You will put yourself in the place of knowing where to show up, showing up, facing things that challenge you, meeting those challenges, and then promising yourself to the work of a lifetime.

I'm making this sound simple because you are the only one who can decide what happens next. You might choose to meet challenges, you may not. You might choose to know love, you may not. But with Aphrodite, you can have an ally that will sing your praises and will hold your hand and who will laugh until you remember yourself again.

\* \* \*

No matter what aspect of Aphrodite calls to you in this moment, She might have something to offer you. You might move from aspect to aspect to find what you need, and you might move into a ritual and into something completely new with Her by your side. You might engage with Her in a way that is personal and private and surprising. I know I have.

# Chapter 9

# Cultivating a Relationship with Her

Just as with any being, divine or not, building a relationship takes time. It takes showing up for the other, getting to know them, following through on promises to them, and being ready to make amends when they need to be made. I imagine that building relationships with any deity could look a lot like this list below, and I've brought in some magickal practices that I do or have done, as well as some things that Aphrodite has told me about building a relationship with Her.

## Getting to Know You

One of the first things to do is to learn the stories of Aphrodite. And even if you know them, it is wise to read them regularly to deepen into what they mean, how the stories support your personal context of working with this goddess, and what they might reveal to you, depending on the place you are in your life right now.

One thing that worked well for me was to read a story at every new moon and then allow it to grow in me until the full moon. Then use the waning moon period to think about what I learned, to journal on it, and to find ways to bring those lessons into my life. The more you read the stories, the more it will help to find different versions of the stories as told by different authors. Find ones that are translations and then find other translations to see how the stories move and shift. The more you know, the more you will know Her. And while there are always mysteries that are not written down, making the effort to get to know the godds seems to have its own rewards.

It's a process of coming to understanding and depth, like asking questions on a first date. Where do you come from?

What have you experienced? What do you know about yourself? What have you explored? Who did you interact with? Who are your parents? Who were your previous lovers? What are the ways that you came into your power? When did you make mistakes? What have you learned? For me, the process of learning about the stories is the place of stepping away from preconceived notions and building a relationship that offers the path to intimacy.

## Making Space

If there's something that seems to be true about working with Aphrodite, it is that She loves beauty. She loves spaces for Her presence and physical spaces of contact. I find Her to be the one who wants to have altars in every place possible. Much like other godds I've worked with, She wants to be celebrated and present in living and working spaces. She wants to be worshipped and loved.

To do this, I created a space for Her in my bedroom, which was the natural space of Her presence. In the space of love and connection, She wanted to be clearly felt and established. While your relationship may be different than mine, I hold the cultivation of relationship as setting the space for arrival. And once She had one place in my home, She was keen to have more places. She showed up in my bathroom, in the living room, by a stone shell that was a part of the property when I moved in. She wanted to be on a table, by the hearth, and in smaller spaces where piles of seashells emerged.

These spaces have changed over time. As my work with Her has deepened, I began to make offerings of wine and chocolate. I bought Her roses and roses and more roses. Indeed, She also led me to an altar cloth made of artificial pearls. And She wanted more pearls, the ones that were rough and shining. I have noticed She needs more space than other deities. She likes Her image to be present in statues and oyster shells. She asks that I bring Her more gifts and beautiful things. She's wanted a picture of me and my lover close by.

I've left Her notes under mirrors and I've brought Her pearl necklaces that sometimes arrived at unexpected times. She beckons certain colors and shades and textures. She offers the possibility of beauty in all corners of my world. And when I bring Her what She delights in, I feel Her smile and warmth wash over me.

## Daily Practices

I find it important to bring the godds into my daily practices. This brings attention and presence into each day. While this has evolved over time, I have noticed She is particularly keen on things like:

Baths
Anointing
Songs
Prayers
Sensual touch

For some time, there was a call for me to do sacred baths with Her on my mind. She wanted me to luxuriate in the radiance of my own being and I was hesitant to take on this challenge. She asked for hot baths with rose petals and milk. I created baths that wrapped my skin in soft belief and scents of love.

The bath I come back to the most is a bath of Epsom salts, rose petals, and rose water. I fill the bath with warm water that is warm enough to hold me for a while. But She doesn't seem to want hot baths as She is less about burning away or aggression and more about inviting the possibility of sinking deeper into beauty. This is less about beauty in the way that society holds this, and more about the feeling of beauty. I could also say this is about the way that we experience the beauty of our unique being. And celebrating this with a bath becomes the portal of understanding and immersion. Beauty is not a thing to hold, but more about an experience to know.

I've also had a daily practice of anointing myself with an oil that has been made specifically with Her in mind. I take a breath and say Her name. I take another breath and say Her name. I take another breath and say Her name. As I do, bring the scent of the oil into my nostrils, I feel the way it dances and plays with the air exchange of me and the world. I then rub the oil into my heart and feel the warmth spread into the spaces of my being. I call into myself the willingness to love for that day. I call into myself the possibility of love in each moment. I call into myself the daring to love when it is hard and seemingly impossible. I call in love to myself. I call in love to others. I call in love for those who might not feel it – and need it.

Another practice I hold is that of sacred song and voice play. I do not have specific songs I *must* use, but I allow myself to sing to Her as though I were singing in Her temple. And I hold that the world is Her temple and my voice is the way to stretch out the love of my heart. I sing sweetly and earnestly, sometimes with words and sometimes with sounds. I feel into my heart's experience and my heart's desire, allowing it to be a spell, a love spell. I sing until the song feels done or my body feels full of brightness. I sing of beauty and I sing for the ways that I can know myself to be beautiful too.

Like the creation of song, I also bring into the space spontaneous prayers. I might offer prayers to Her of gratitude. I might offer prayers that request help and support. I pray to the ways that She is wise and understanding and patient. I pray to Aphrodite that the world might know beauty and love. I pray to Her for the darkness of my experience to know clarity. I pray to Her about the things I have seen and the wonder I have known. I thank Her for the opportunities to love and the courage to take the risk to love. I pray for the wisdom to know how to love myself and others more fully. I pray to the delight of Her smile.

Another prayer I have used is to witness my own beauty. Coming from a background in which outside appearances were everything, I have spent a long time dismantling the ways in which that has caused me to become disillusioned in this world. I have internalized those messages of 'not enough' and 'not as pretty as _____' and She helps me push them aside.

In Her name, I have looked at myself in the mirror and reminded myself of the beautiful parts of myself. I have named all of the things I can see, as well as all of the things I have done to encourage beauty in the world. My mouth is beautiful. My legs are beautiful. The way I take care of my body is an act of worship. The way I speak to those I love is an act of devotion. I am a beautiful person on any day, no matter what I do. I am a flower that is blooming and wilting and coming back to life. I am an ocean wave that arrives and leaves and returns.

Sometimes I will incorporate sensual touch into my daily practice. While this has included self-pleasure or bringing Her energy into sex, it is often more about delighting in my own skin. I might trace the line of my neck with my fingers or feel the way my ribcage spreads below my breasts. I may stroke my breastbone and know my heart to be beating there. Or I might hold my lover closely and trace their lips.

I have also brought into each day the practice of knowing beauty. This might be as simple as sighing when I see something that delights me. Or it might be as complicated as going out into nature to discover what is beautiful about that particular day. I try to find, even in the toughest of days, something that makes me remember that the world is not ugly. And She is with me. She reminds me that I too am a part of that beauty.

## Conversation & Silence

In building a relationship, I had to make new priorities. I needed to move away from some things to make space for Her. This has meant working more intensely with Her than with other godds at times, as the relationship needed that attention.

I would find a space where I could be quiet, often in front of an altar of hers and I would be silent. I might begin with the thought of opening myself up to Her, but then I would allow myself to just be in Her presence. Over time, this has become easier and less detailed in its practice, but it started with invocations to Her or prayers to Her that I found. I found I needed to beckon Her to be present, and then I would be silent. And sometimes, I would feel and hear nothing. And sometimes, I would feel and hear so much.

I vacillate between silence and conversation, which might look the same from the outside if someone were watching. I close my eyes and let things arrive in my experience. I might linger and wait to see what happens. And it could take a long time before noticing anything.

Sometimes, I let myself go into a trance-like state with music or with some sort of wordless chant. And as I drop into that space, I hear what needs to be heard. Sometimes, it feels right to ask questions. Sometimes, it is clear I need to just listen or experience. Sometimes, it's not words or answers. It's the way a muscle relaxes or the way the air feels on my skin. Sometimes it comes later in a dream. Sometimes it comes weeks later as a distinct moment of knowing an answer.

As time has gone on, I've talked with Aphrodite during the day. I talk to Her like a friend and a wise one. I ask questions, I share thoughts, and I might even challenge any replies I received. And I know it is Her because there is a presence that is clearly not me and it is consistent in its energetic tone. I know it because I've showed up before and it has arrived. I recognize Her. I know Her.

Just as relationships are, sometimes there is silence. Sometimes I am awkward and the 'logical' part of me thinks I'm making things up. And sometimes I am. Even then, I still feel the ways in which the relationship is progressing. Not every interaction will be the most amazing I've ever had. And not every conversation will be the one that answers all of my questions. Sometimes, you just sit in the silence and the unknowing. Sometimes, you have to continue to show up because this creates the trust that partnerships need.

## Creation

While some say that Aphrodite is a goddess of fertility, I might look at that as creation in one's life versus childbirth. With that in mind, getting creative with Aphrodite is a lovely way to connect. Some ways might include:

**Creating a girdle** – Texts have talked about a magical girdle that Aphrodite owned that inspired passion and brought back together disputing lovers. You can also create a girdle that will bring back your own love to yourself, perhaps bringing together those quarrelling parts of yourself so that you might feel peace. You can make this with threads, as outlined in Jane Meredith's book 'Aphrodite's Magic: Celebrating and Healing Your Sexuality,' or you could use your intuition to make a magical belt that allows you to be fully in your power of creation.

**Collages** – Bringing together pictures that are beautiful to you can also be in devotion to Aphrodite. You might find pictures of nature or of lovers or of other things that make you feel loved. In this practice, you might create a collage for a specific purpose. Maybe you want to bring love back into your relationship or you want to bring love back into yourself. Whatever you choose, you can create these collages, placing them on your altar with Aphrodite. She can watch over them and send Her love to them.

**Sculpting** – It can be helpful to use your hands in some

way when you offer creation as devotion to Aphrodite. In this way, you feel the strength of your hands as they make something into something else. You can smooth the clay into a heart and then fill it with a breath of love. You can sing to the heart or tell the heart what you need, and if you're using quick-dry clay, the drying action will bring those promises and breath into the clay where it will hold power for you. You might decide to bring this heart around with you or you might decide to put it on an altar.

**Altars** – While this has already been mentioned, it bears repeating. Aphrodite likes altars. She likes to feel there are temples in Her name. When you create altars, remember what She loves and add to it what you feel is beautiful too. Bring your beauty together.

If you notice any resistance around creation, allow yourself to let go of the outcomes. Beauty doesn't have to look a certain way or be a certain thing. No one else but you needs to find the beauty in something you have created. The act of creation itself is beauty. The act of taking a moment to create just for the sake of creating is beauty.

## Love Letters

One of my favorite practices with Aphrodite is to write a love letter to myself, to the world, and to whatever needs a little extra love. In one class I took, we made Valentine's Day cards for ourselves with wishes and kisses. Using colored paper and other decorations, we spent time thinking about what we would like to hear in a card we received. You can deepen into your memory into the messages you heard about love and the ways that it wasn't met or understood.

Stop and think about what you might want to hear from someone else and give yourself the gift instead of waiting for it.

You are loved.
You are precious.
You are beautiful.
I will not abandon you.
I am here for you.
I love you.
You are enough.

And spend some time making this card just the way you'd like it. You might turn on beautiful music or you might do this in silence. Spend all the time you need to feel like the card is complete and EXACTLY what you want. Stop and read it to yourself. Allow yourself to feel the feelings you feel. Laugh. Cry. Sigh. And put this card in a place where it will be safe and private. Read it so often that you can see it in your mind without opening your eyes.

Give yourself the gift of everything that you deserve to hear and everything you deserve to feel. When you feel the card is done, you can choose to burn it or bury it in the yard as a gift to the earth (assuming it's made from earth-friendly materials).

## Mirror Work

One of the most challenging things I've done in all of my work with Aphrodite is mirror work. For so long, I was told I was not good enough and that I needed to change my body in order to be beautiful. As a result, mirrors became difficult to approach. They would always show me what I believed from others. They would distort my face and my body and they would reveal that I was never going to be good enough.

In truth, mirrors aren't true. While they give us a reflection of ourselves, they are distorted by the messages in our mind and the actual reversal of the image. We will never see ourselves just as we are. We only see ourselves in what is reflected back.

One practice that you can use to bring yourself closer to your own beauty and to Her is to create a mirror. Find a mirror that you can decorate and adorn with things that you find beautiful. You might decorate it with pearls, with seashells, or with other bits that make you smile. Find ways to bring decadence and delight to the mirror so you see it and want to hold it.

Once you have the mirror decorated, spend time each day looking at your reflection. For some, this might mean looking at your reflection and then looking away before you can return to the image. For others, this might be a simple practice. Start where you are. Start where you are on that day.

Commit to a few minutes of gazing into your reflection to see yourself just as you are. As you become more comfortable, you might start to tell yourself 'I love you' and 'You are beauty.' Find a phrase that allows you to bring yourself present into yourself. Give yourself permission to have this be a healing practice, one that brings you closer to your heart and your center. And should it feel challenging, you can imagine Aphrodite is beside you, touching your shoulder, and urging you to look deeper.

### Ocean Devotion

If Aphrodite was born on sea foam, it only makes sense to meet Her there, to meet Her at the place of beginning and creation. If you are not able to make it to an ocean, there are other practices you can follow to bring the ocean to your heart. (Other bodies of water work too!)

Ocean offerings – One of the practices I do most often is to leave offerings for Aphrodite at the ocean. These are always natural offerings that can decompose and that do not pollute the waters. I often bring organically grown roses or some other flower, throwing them into the waves or leaving them at the shore for Her to 'collect.' I will bless the flower with my love or with some other prayer I want to send to Aphrodite.
Love letters – It can also be healing to write prayers to

Aphrodite on the sand, so they can be swept up by the waves. You might draw hearts or write words. Or you might create a symbol that encompasses what you want to say, what you want heard.

**Cleansing** – If you are in a place where you want to let go and give something to Aphrodite to hold or heal, you might step into the ocean for cleansing. You might wash your hands, your hair, your heart, and your feet to remove what needs to be removed. Or you might dunk yourself completely in the water.

**Wave immersion** – When you're not near an ocean or large body of water, you can always bring to mind the image of an ocean. If it helps, there are many sources of ocean wave sounds on the internet that can carry you into that setting. Find a safe place, get comfortable, and allow the waves to crash over the places that need touch. Send flowers out to Her, send holy whispers to Her.

The ocean is a place of beginnings and movement, a place of coming in and moving out. In the place of Her creation, you may also find your birth.

## Aphrodite Writing

While I would say that aspecting is a deep way to come into relationship with a godd, it is also not something to do without training and supervision. Holding the energy of a deity can be delightful, and it can also be hard on a body and mind that are not prepared. (I know not everyone believes in such caution, but I'm going to err on the side of 'don't do it' unless you have aspected before.) With that said, there are other ways to bring yourself into the presence of a deity to begin to forge a relationship. Like so many magickal practices, it begins with finding yourself in a space that is safe and secure.

Allow yourself to become present, letting go of anything that might be a distraction. You might imagine yourself breathing out the distractions and breathing in presence. Others might enjoy imagining roots dropping down into the Earth from the soles of their feet, reaching down to connect with the center of the Earth before rising up and up to connect with the vastness of the sky and universe before coming back down into the place of will or heart.

Once you feel settled, grab a journal or paper and a pen. Write down a few questions you might want to ask Aphrodite. Once you're done, set these beside you. Close your eyes and picture Aphrodite in your mind, however you imagine Her to look. Call Her up into your mind until you begin to feel what She feels like. Take your time here. Once you do, allow your eyes to open partially, as though you were seeing the world with Her eyes. Feel the way She feels; allowing it to travel down your head and your throat and down into your heart. Let Her energy travel the length of your arms and into your hand that takes the pen.

Allow and trust your hand to write the answers to your questions with Aphrodite's guidance. If you start to judge what the words say, take a breath and let that judgment go. Let the words fall onto the page.

Once you have completed the writing, give yourself another moment or two to think about what might need to be said, and then take some deep breaths. Thank Aphrodite for Her wisdom and with each breath out, feel Her presence leaving you. Feel the energy that was once dripping down your body begin to dry or to disappear.

Shake your body and open your eyes so you are in the room and present in your human body. You might want some water or to eat a snack to ground further before reading what has been given to you in this writing exercise.

It might be helpful to complete this exercise with questions about Aphrodite, Her life, and Her history. This can help you learn more about how She presents herself to you personally.

You might also find out information that may not have come through books. Keep these writings in a special place so you can come back to them. You might even go back to these writings and ask the questions again to see what happens in the future as the relationship deepens.

If you are concerned that what you have written is 'you' and not 'Her,' this is completely fine. And you should let that go. There are certainly times when you will be informed more by where you are in your life and those thoughts will come to the surface – and this is also information that can be helpful to you.

* * *

Building a relationship with Aphrodite is a beautiful process, an ongoing practice, and a commitment. It is showing up again and again, even in silence and even in pain. Know that She will hold you.

# Conclusion

*"Fairest of stars, that with your persant light*
*And with the cherishing of your streames clear,*
*Causen in love heartes to be light*
*Only through shining of your glad sphere,*
*Now laud and praise, O Venus, lady dear,*
*Be to your name, that have withoute sin*
*This man fortuned his lady for to win."*
–John Lydgate, monk, 14<sup>th</sup> century

The beauty of Aphrodite comes not from Her skin or the way flowers arose when She stepped on the shore. The wonder of Aphrodite comes from the presence that She offers, the changing ways to look at the way a heart beats and who it beats for.

With all of Her aspects and stories, She continues to offer insights and opportunities to know Her and to know ourselves better. For what is the world without love? How can we live without love? If we can continuously meet Her and meet the way She shows up unapologetically, we may too be able to step forward from our own ocean onto the shore of a fuller, richer life.

Aphrodite offers love and beauty, but also initiation. She offers initiation into the mysteries of love, the way it is everything we want and sometimes everything we fear. She tells us and shows us that the way to a heart is through the everyday actions, the everyday words, and the promise to show up fully as ourselves.

She shows us that we can have stories and faults and missteps and still emerge.
She tells us that we can be beauty and we are beauty, in all of our days.
She reminds us that the way of magick and wonder is love.

I imagine that if you are here right now, you have already heard Her call. I imagine She has already tapped on your shoulder or whispered in your ear that you need to listen to Her.

And if you're still not sure, I invite you to take a seashell, one that's big enough to cover your ear and listen to the ocean sounds. Allow yourself to deepen into the possibility that She is already here. She is already waiting for you.

May she watch over your heart.
May she bless your relationships.
May she continue to offer you peace, solace, and laughter.

Blessed be.

# Resources & Bibliography

*Aphrodite and Venus in Myth & Mimesis*, Nora Clark

*Aphrodite's Magic: Celebrate and Heal Your Sexuality*, Jane Meredith

*Aphrodite's Priestess*, Laurelei Black

*Aphrodite: The Mythology of Cyprus*, Stass Paraskos

*Aphrodite: The Origins and History of the Greek Goddess of Love*, Edited by Andrew Scott & Charles River

*Cult of Aphrodite*, Laurelei Black

*From Ishtar to Aphrodite: 3200 Years of Cypriot Hellenism, Treasures from the Museums of Cyprus*, Dr. Sophocles Hadjisavvas

*Goddesses of Sun and Moon*, Karl Kerenyi

*Greek Religion*, Walter Burkert

*Hesiod: Theogony and Words and Days*, Translated by M.L West

*Lost Goddesses of Early Greece: A Collection of Pre-Hellenic Myths*, Charlene Spretnak

*Mythology*, Edith Hamilton

*Mythopedia: She's All That*, Megan E. Bryant

*Pagan Meditations: The Worlds of Aphrodite, Artemis, and Hestia*, Ginette Paris

*The Goddess of Love*, Geoffrey Grigson

*The Greek Myths*, Robert Graves

*The Iliad*, Homer

*The Meaning of Aphrodite*, Paul Friedrich

*Women in Greek Myth*, Mary R. Lefkowitz

*Worshipping Aphrodite: Art & Cult in Classical Athens*, Rachel Rosenzweig

https://www.theoi.com/Olympios/Aphrodite.html

https://en.wikipedia.org/wiki/Aphrodite

https://www.ancient.eu/Aphrodite/

https://www.britannica.com/topic/Aphrodite-Greek-mythology

https://www.theravenswingmagicalco.com/events-oakland/2018/1/12/temple-of-aphrodite-x94ep

**MOON
BOOKS**

## PAGANISM & SHAMANISM

What is Paganism? A religion, a spirituality, an alternative
belief system, nature worship? You can find support for all these
definitions (and many more) in dictionaries, encyclopaedias, and
text books of religion, but subscribe to any one and the truth will
evade you. Above all Paganism is a creative pursuit, an encounter
with reality, an exploration of meaning and an expression of the
soul. Druids, Heathens, Wiccans and others, all contribute their
insights and literary riches to the Pagan tradition. Moon Books
invites you to begin or to deepen your own encounter, right here,
right now.
If you have enjoyed this book, why not tell other readers by
posting a review on your preferred book site.

**Recent bestsellers from Moon Books are:**

**Journey to the Dark Goddess**
How to Return to Your Soul
Jane Meredith
Discover the powerful secrets of the Dark Goddess and
transform your depression, grief and pain into healing
and integration.
Paperback: 978-1-84694-677-6 ebook: 978-1-78099-223-5

**Shamanic Reiki**
Expanded Ways of Working with Universal Life Force Energy
Llyn Roberts, Robert Levy
Shamanism and Reiki are each powerful ways of healing; together,
their power multiplies. *Shamanic Reiki* introduces techniques to
help healers and Reiki practitioners tap ancient healing wisdom.
Paperback: 978-1-84694-037-8 ebook: 978-1-84694-650-9

**Pagan Portals – The Awen Alone**
Walking the Path of the Solitary Druid
Joanna van der Hoeven
An introductory guide for the solitary Druid, *The Awen Alone* will
accompany you as you explore, and seek out your own place
within the natural world.
Paperback: 978-1-78279-547-6 ebook: 978-1-78279-546-9

**A Kitchen Witch's World of Magical Herbs & Plants**
Rachel Patterson
A journey into the magical world of herbs and plants, filled with
magical uses, folklore, history and practical magic. By popular
writer, blogger and kitchen witch, Tansy Firedragon.
Paperback: 978-1-78279-621-3 ebook: 978-1-78279-620-6

**Medicine for the Soul**
The Complete Book of Shamanic Healing
Ross Heaven
All you will ever need to know about shamanic healing and how to
become your own shaman...
Paperback: 978-1-78099-419-2 ebook: 978-1-78099-420-8


**Shaman Pathways – The Druid Shaman**
Exploring the Celtic Otherworld
Danu Forest
A practical guide to Celtic shamanism with exercises and
techniques as well as traditional lore for exploring the Celtic
Otherworld.
Paperback: 978-1-78099-615-8 ebook: 978-1-78099-616-5


**Traditional Witchcraft for the Woods and Forests**
A Witch's Guide to the Woodland with Guided Meditations and
Pathworking
Mélusine Draco
A Witch's guide to walking alone in the woods, with guided
meditations and pathworking.
Paperback: 978-1-84694-803-9 ebook: 978-1-84694-804-6


**Wild Earth, Wild Soul**
A Manual for an Ecstatic Culture
Bill Pfeiffer
Imagine a nature-based culture so alive and so connected,
spreading like wildfire. This book is the first flame...
Paperback: 978-1-78099-187-0 ebook: 978-1-78099-188-7

## Naming the Goddess
Trevor Greenfield
*Naming the Goddess* is written by over eighty adherents and scholars of Goddess and Goddess Spirituality.
Paperback: 978-1-78279-476-9 ebook: 978-1-78279-475-2

## Shapeshifting into Higher Consciousness
Heal and Transform Yourself and Our World with Ancient Shamanic and Modern Methods
Llyn Roberts
Ancient and modern methods that you can use every day to transform yourself and make a positive difference in the world.
Paperback: 978-1-84694-843-5 ebook: 978-1-84694-844-2

Readers of ebooks can buy or view any of these bestsellers by clicking on the live link in the title. Most titles are published in paperback and as an ebook. Paperbacks are available in traditional bookshops. Both print and ebook formats are available online.

Find more titles and sign up to our readers' newsletter at http://www.johnhuntpublishing.com/paganism
Follow us on Facebook at https://www.facebook.com/MoonBooks
and Twitter at https://twitter.com/MoonBooksJHP